299.

The Decorative Art of

Limoges

Porcelain and Boxes

Keith and Thomas Waterbrook-Clyde

4880 Lower Valley Road, Atglen, PA 19310 USA

Dedication

We dedicate this book to the many named and unnamed French and American artists who were responsible for the decorative art of Limoges porcelain and also to our good friend, Yasumasa Tanano, who has helped us in numerous ways.

Waterbrook-Clyde, Keith.
    The decorative art of Limoges : porcelain and boxes / Keith and Thomas Waterbrook-Clyde
        p.   cm.
    Includes bibliographical references and index.
    ISBN 0-7643-0802-5 (hardcover)
    1. Limoges porcelain. 2. China painting--France--Limoges. I. Waterbrook-Clyde, Thomas. II. Title. III. Title: Limoges.
    NK4399.L5W38   1999
    738.2'0944'66--dc21   99-12050
                                                       CIP

Design by Blair Loughrey
Type set in Vivaldi/Geometric 415/Souvenir

ISBN: 0-7643-0802-5
Printed in China
1 2 3 4

Published by Schiffer Publishing Ltd.
4880 Lower Valley Road
Atglen, PA 19310
Phone: (610) 593-1777; Fax: (610) 593-2002
E-mail: Schifferbk@aol.com
Please visit our web site catalog at
www.schifferbooks.com

This book may be purchased from the publisher.
Include $3.95 for shipping.
Please try your bookstore first.
We are interested in hearing from authors
with book ideas on related subjects.
You may write for a free catalog.

In Europe, Schiffer books are distributed by
Bushwood Books
6 Marksbury Rd.
Kew Gardens
Surrey TW9 4JF England
Phone: 44 (0)181 392-8585; Fax: 44 (0)181 392-9876
E-mail: Bushwd@aol.com

Contents

Acknowledgments

There have been many individuals who have assisted us in numerous ways with the development of this book on Limoges porcelain.

Special recognition goes to Lucy Zahran, who pointed us in the right directions from the very start and who graciously let us photograph many fine porcelain pieces from her stores on Rodeo Drive in Beverly Hills and in South Coast Plaza in Costa Mesa, California.

Also of very special help to us was Yasumasa Tanano, who drew all the company marks that we were unable to photograph, who let us photograph many pieces of his extensive porcelain collection, and who has served us many fine Japanese dinners. Best of all, Mr. Tanano has become a very close friend. He is a member of the Haviland Collectors Internationale Foundation.

Special thanks also goes to Bruce Guilmette for giving us the opportunity to photograph his extensive and very fine porcelain collection. He and his partner, Allan Ward, graciously gave up a weekend to let us visit their home.

JoAnn Williams took the time to search among her Haviland collection for non-Haviland Limoges pieces for us to photograph. Mrs. Williams is the editor of the newsletter of the Haviland Collectors Internationale Foundation. Jacqueline Lowensteiner, who also, like ourselves, collects both older Limoges pieces as well as Limoges boxes, provided us with many photographs for this book. Dorla Battersby gave us free access to her showcases to photograph as many pieces as we wished. Tom Roth answered our ad in the Haviland newsletter and was kind enough to send us several photographs of pieces from his collection.

Leny R. Davidson, president of Chamart Exclusives Inc., New York City, provided us with an overview of Limoges boxes and shared information about the history of the company founded by her uncle, Charles Martine. She also sent us several photographs of boxes for this book. Margaret L. Wilmerding, sales manager for Artoria, New York City, shared with us the manufacturing process of Limoges porcelain boxes and also provided us with information on Artoria, while extending an invitation to us to visit their manufacturing company in Limoges. Laurence de La Grange, manager, Atelier Le Tallec, Paris, France, gave us background information on her company and invited us to Paris to photograph the company's extensive collection. Shirley Dickersen, president of S&D Limoges, Texas, graciously sent us several pictures of her Limoges boxes, which we were able to include in this book. Hélène Huret, Bernardaud, Paris, France, provided information on Bernardaud as well as information on Ancienne Manufacture Royale. Richard Sonking from Rochard, New York City, sent us several Limoges boxes, which we photographed for this book.

Corrine Arnaud, Los Angeles, was key to our research efforts. She provided valuable information by researching and translating background information on Limoges companies and other key information that was only available from material written in French. Jack Vartabedian of Hooper Camera in North Hollywood, California, provided consistent advice on improving our photographic techniques, encouraged us when everything seemed to go wrong and reprinted, when necessary, our rolls of film.

Finally, in our tracing of the histories of several Limoges companies and the dating of their porcelain and decorating marks, we are heavily indebted to the research of a number of individuals who have published material on these subjects. We have relied heavily on the works of Jean d'Albis and Céleste Romanet, Mary Frank Gaston, Elisabeth Cameron and J. P. Cushion, whose works are cited in the Bibliography. Special thanks also to the Haviland Collectors Internationale Foundation and Wallace J. Tomasini, Ph.D., for allowing us to use the chart of Haviland marks and dates and for background information on the decoration of Limoges porcelain and to Jean d'Albis for allowing us to use the Haviland family tree.

Introduction

We became Limoges collectors by chance. Shopping for a wedding present for a friend who collects Limoges boxes, we decided on a Limoges box wedding cake for a gift. We got hooked. Shortly thereafter, during a trip to London, we began cruising Harrods, Harvey Nichols, Asprey's and other stores for Limoges boxes. After returning home, we started looking in antiques malls where we began to notice beautiful old pieces of Limoges porcelain. Not being able to choose between contemporary Limoges boxes and old Limoges porcelain, we had no choice but to collect both. And that's how this book came into being.

We collect all kinds of Limoges porcelain—old and new; different shapes and subjects; decorative and non-decorative items; hand-painted pieces, white wares and pieces decorated with transfers; and pieces manufactured and decorated by all of the different Limoges companies throughout the years. This book includes mostly older Limoges pieces (1950 and earlier) and then moves to contemporary Limoges boxes. As a result, this book might at first appear to be about two different topics—older pieces and contemporary boxes. In some sense this may be true, but in another broader sense the topics are similar. The porcelain for both originates in Limoges, some from the same factories; much of the decorating for both is done in France; and both exhibit fine examples of exquisite painting and decoration, some of which is in the same traditions.

There are some dissimilarities, however, especially in terms of the appeal or "art" of the two topics. Most of the examples of older Limoges porcelain, especially those available to the average collector, are limited to a few basic porcelain shapes—plates, vases, dresser items, dinnerware, etc. The paintings and transfers on these pieces are one dimensional, although additional decorative accents may include, depending on the item, handles, legs, bases and so on. Many contemporary Limoges boxes, on the other hand, are appealing because they combine unique porcelain shapes, which are three dimensional replications of the subject, with decorative painting and hardware. We call these "subject" boxes, because the shape of the box identifies the subject. For example, to portray a cherub on a piece of older Limoges porcelain, the cherub would actually have to be painted or a transfer set on the surface of the porcelain; whereas with the contemporary box, the box itself would already be molded in the shape of a cherub.

These two distinct designs have somewhat different implications. Because for the most part older Limoges porcelain must rely on the quality of the painting alone to generate appeal, the panting and decoration is oftentimes more intricate and lavish. Much more detail is included in the painting to communicate the "feel" or expression of the subject. With subject boxes, on the other hand, we get a good sense of the object just by its shape; and, as a result, oftentimes less attention is paid to the quality of the painting, although this is certainly not the case with many of the finer boxes. There are, of course, many "traditional" boxes—those that are round, oval, rectangle, etc.—which do not rely on shape to convey their subject matter. Many of these traditional boxes, incidentally, represent some of the best examples of contemporary hand-painted boxes.

The material that we have selected to include in this collector's book reflects our own personal interests as well as takes into account current published material on Limoges porcelain. Our primary interests in older Limoges porcelain are in well decorated art objects, often in the shapes of chargers, plaques and vases, and pieces that are unusual either in terms of shape or in manufacturing/decorating origin. For example, many of the most highly decorated pieces of Limoges porcelain are of game subjects, so we have included many photographs of pieces with hand-painted game animals. On the other hand, we have included relatively fewer photographs of pieces from regular dinnerware sets, since we are not experts in pattern identification and since this is a broad enough subject that it needs to be addressed separately. Haviland dinnerware, for example, is well illustrated and documented by Nora Travis in her book, *Haviland China: The Age of Elegance*.

Our photographs of contemporary Limoges boxes are limited to pieces that are, for the most part, well decorated. All of the boxes are decorated in France and most are entirely hand-painted. We have not attempted to provide photographs which fully represent the breadth of shapes and subjects, since these literally number in the thousands. We have, for example, included several photographs of Le Tallec boxes, which, although very limited in number, do represent some of the most exquisite examples of hand-painted porcelain in France. We have also included many more photographs of boxes from Chamart, S&D Limoges, Rochard and Artoria, since these companies offer some of the best examples of fine hand-painted Limoges boxes that are much more readily available to collectors.

A note about captions: For each photograph, we have provided the name of the item and the dimensions. When available, we have given the name and mark number of the decorating studio, the name and mark number of the porcelain manufacturer, and the name of the artist. Finally, we have included the estimated value.

Part I.

Limoges Porcelain

History of Limoges Porcelain

The formula for manufacturing of hard-paste porcelain in Europe was first learned by the Germans in the early part of the 18th century, and they produced the first piece of porcelain around 1730. It was not until about 35 years later, in 1764 or 1765, that clay containing kaolin and feldspar, the key ingredients of hard-paste porcelain, was discovered at Saint Yrieix in the Limoges region of France, located 200 miles southwest of Paris on the Vienne River. In about 1770, Anne Robert Jacques Turgot, who was then the chief government official in Limoges, recognized the importance of these clay deposits and the future potential of porcelain production to the city and region. At this time, there was a pottery factory in Limoges which had been producing pottery, or faience, since 1736. Turgot now began urging the head of this pottery factory, André Massié, to change from making pottery to manufacturing porcelain. As a result of Turgot's urging, Massié partnered with two wealthy Limoges men, the Grellet brothers, to work on refining the manufacturing of hard-paste porcelain. Massié and the Grellet brothers were assisted in this effort by a chemist named Fournérat. Their initial efforts at making porcelain were being carried out clandestinely because at this point in time, porcelain production in France was limited by royal edict to King Louis XV's factory at Sèvres and other Paris factories. Because of Turgot's continuing support and influence—Turgot later became the Finance Minister for King Louis XVI—the Grellet factory finally received recognition as a porcelain manufacturer when, in 1773, it obtained an exemption from the export tax, received an annual subsidy of 3,000 francs for 10 years and the right to use the porcelain mark, C.D., for the Comte d'Artois, King Louis XVI's brother and future King Charles X. Several years later, in 1784, King Louis XVI bought the Grellet company and made it a subsidiary of his factory at Sèvres, at which time the Grellet factory also began using the Sèvres mark, which contained the word royalle. Although the younger Grellet brother continued to remain director of the factory, he was replaced as director four years later, in 1788, by François Alluaud. The mark, C.D., indicating the factory was under the protection of the Comte d'Artois, was used from approximately 1773 to 1796.

At about the same time that the Grellet company started, porcelain production also began—about 1774—in La Seynie, near Limoges, when the Château of Seynie was turned into a porcelain factory. During the early years of porcelain production in Limoges and La Seynie, the porcelain pastes were sold directly to other factories. In fact, most of the factories in Paris bought the raw material for porcelain from companies in Limoges and La Seynie. In addition to selling porcelain paste, these companies also sold undecorated porcelain blanks to other factories both within France and to other European countries. The earliest existing piece of Limoges porcelain was made in 1771. For the first 25 years, the factories produced ivory colored porcelain which was generally decorated with little flowers, and the colors themselves were usually somewhat dull.

It was not, however, until the end of the French Revolution in 1799, when all restrictions on porcelain manufacturing were lifted, that the porcelain industry in Limoges really got started. By 1830 the manufacturing of porcelain was becoming an important industry; and by about 1870 the manufacturing process had been perfected and the decoration was much more sophisticated. The story is told that in 1839 a lady went to the New York City store owned by Daniel and David Haviland to inquire if they could match a porcelain cup, which she had purchased in France. The Havilands were so impressed by the superiority of the French porcelain over the English china which they sold in their store that David Haviland subsequently went to France to inquire about the production of French porcelain. The Havilands wanted the companies in Limoges to produce French porcelain in the shapes and decorating styles of English china. When the Limoges companies were not responsive to these suggestions, David Haviland founded his own porcelain factory in Limoges, which proved later to be responsible for the commercial success of Limoges porcelain. The Haviland company perfected the kilns, introduced lithography and engraving to the decorating process, and mechanized much of the manufacturing process. By 1886, the Haviland company was responsible for about 10 percent of all porcelain production in Limoges. At this time there were a total of 35 porcelain manufacturers employing about 5,000 people and 62 decorating studios employing about 2,000 people.

Manufacturing and Decorating of Limoges Porcelain

Limoges hard-paste porcelain, called *pâte duré* or *grand feu* in French, is some of the world's finest porcelain. Because of several of its properties, porcelain is considered superior to both earthenware and stoneware. Porcelain does not develop crazing and is translucent, lighter, more delicate in appearance, more durable, and nonporous (meaning it cannot be penetrated by liquid or other potentially harmful substances). While materials for making earthenware and stoneware are available in many places throughout the world, only a few places, such as Limoges, France, contain deposits of kaolin, a natural ingredient for making porcelain. Both the porcelain and the enamel are made from a mixture of kaolin, quartz and feldspar, although the proportions of these materials are different for each. Kaolin is responsible for giving porcelain its "structure" and its whiteness, quartz provides the translucency and hardness, and feldspar is the "blending" agent which allows glazing.

There are basically two methods now for producing porcelain—*calibrating and casting*. Calibrating is used to describe the process where the soft paste for a plate, for example, is placed on a plaster mold that is rotating on a machine. Calibers are then used to press the paste against the mold to form the plate. Frequently, however, rather than using a soft paste, a powder mixture is substituted and the piece is formed using extreme pressure. In the latter case, the mold is made of resin instead of plaster and drying is not required.

Casting refers to a process that uses liquid soft paste and a mold to form the porcelain. This process, which has made Limoges porcelain famous, is used for making such pieces as boxes and vases. The soft paste is poured into a mold, and once it reaches the desired thickness, the excess paste is poured out. The blank itself is then removed from the mold, after reaching the required hardness, and allowed to dry.

The porcelain blank is now fired at 800 to 900 degrees C to completely dry it before applying the enamel. The blank is then dipped into a clear enamel mixture and then fired again at 1400 degrees C for 12 hours and then cooled for another 12 hours before it is removed from the kiln. Because porcelain shrinks about 13 to 15 percent during this last major firing process, each blank is slightly different in shape. This is why, for example, the rim of a punch bowl may not be exactly even all the way around and why the brass hardware, in the case of boxes, must be fitted by hand— because no two boxes are exactly the same.

After the first firing, the blank is called bisque, which means that the enamel has not been applied. Many examples of bisque porcelain are seen, especially in the form of figurines. In some cases, the blanks may be partially decorated before the enamel is applied, and in other cases after the enamel is applied. Additionally, blanks may receive more than one coat of enamel.

The process of decorating porcelain that is entirely hand-painted also requires multiple steps. Because different colors require different firing temperatures, each piece of porcelain may be fired several times, depending upon the number of colors used. Blues and purples require firing temperatures from 750 to 900 degrees C, while reds cannot be fired higher than 550 to 700 degrees C because they will be burned away. Gold is the last color to be applied because it is the most sensitive to firing temperatures. In cases where hand-painting has been applied before the enamel, blues and browns have been the most common colors.

In the earliest traditions, porcelain was painted entirely by hand, with the painter using models to paint the subjects. Around 1855, however, engraved transfers were introduced and later, beginning around 1872, full color lithographic transfers were employed, which accommodated a much broader range of colors and definition. The use of transfers, called *décalomanie*, revolutionized the decoration of porcelain, since by reducing the reliance on the labor intensive method of hand-painting, porcelain could be decorated more inexpensively. Nevertheless, hand-painting was still an important method of decoration; and especially in the more expensive dinnerware patterns, hand applications of colored enamels were used to give emphasis and depth to the transfer subjects. There were also many variations of the use of transfers and hand-painting. Pieces were often outlined with transfers and then filled in by hand-painting; and transfers of, for example, flowers or cherubs or some other subject, were placed against entirely hand-painted backgrounds.

The decoration of boxes requires the one additional step of applying hardware. As stated earlier, because porcelain shrinks during firing, no two pieces of porcelain are exactly the same shape. As a result the brass hardware for boxes is usually applied by hand, and the clasp is then soldered to the hardware. The hardware also comes in several finishes—black, antique, etc.— which are produced by dipping the hardware in different acid compounds.

Qualities of Limoges Porcelain

When we purchase a piece of Limoges porcelain for our collection, we usually buy it because there is something unique about the piece that appeals to us. We can usually define that "something" for ourselves, but we also wanted to know what appeals to other collectors. To find an answer, we have attended and observed numerous auctions and talked with many dealers and collectors. The auctions on the world wide web have been particularly helpful, since you can choose to view only Limoges porcelain, the auctions are occurring continuously and the buyers and sellers represent all regions of the country. There are, of course, regional variations in prices; but based upon our observations over an extended period of time, we have identified the following characteristics which affect Limoges porcelain values:

> Subject matter of decoration
> Age of piece
> Method of decoration—hand-painting,
>   transfers or a mix of hand-painting and
>   transfers
> Artist's signature, if any, and identity of artist
> Quality of decoration or artistic value
> Origin of decoration—French or American
> Size of piece
> Scarcity of a particular blank
> Scarcity of pieces from a particular company
> Completeness of sets
> Overall condition of piece

There is no one characteristic that predominately determines a piece's value; rather, it is usually a combination of factors. The more knowledgeable the Limoges collector, the more likely it is that all of these criteria will come into play at some point, depending on the piece. In putting together the photographs for this book, we have included pieces that will be of interest to a broad range of Limoges collectors, from the new collector to the long-time, seasoned collector. Most of the pieces, with the exceptions of the boxes, are prior to 1950, although there are several exceptions. No pieces from the late 1700s to the early 1800s are included, since most of these items are now mostly found in museums and in some private collections.

IDENTIFYING OBJECTS

In evaluating Limoges porcelain, it is often helpful to determine the purpose of a particular piece. Some pieces are clearly decorative objects, such as chargers, plaques, vases, jardinieres and cachepots. Other pieces are likewise clearly part of a set. Sets include complete dinnerware place settings with serving pieces; specialized dinnerware for serving only game and seafood—fish, birds, oysters and clams; coffee, chocolate and tea sets; dresser sets; and bathroom sets. While the decorative objects are more likely to be lavishly decorated and entirely hand-painted, this is not always the case. Most of the dinnerware is decorated with either transfers or a combination of transfers and hand-painting. On the other hand, many of the dinnerware game sets are highly and skillfully decorated and completely hand-painted, with each plate in the set being slightly different. Many of these plates are decorative objects in themselves. Generally, a complete set, such as a game set with platter, 12 plates and a gravy boat with saucer, command a proportionately higher price since complete, undamaged sets are relatively rare. Since most older sets are incomplete, often with only one or two pieces available, the individual items which once made up the set are now collected as separate, stand alone pieces.

THEMES

The decorative themes and decorating styles of Limoges porcelain covered a wide variety of subjects and styles which have changed over time. For example, figural subjects became popular in the late 1800s around the same time that the French and other Europeans were heavily influenced by Japanese art, *Japonisme*. Game subjects became popular in both the late 1800s and the early 1900s, and there are many examples of fish, shellfish and game dinnerware sets. The very earliest Limoges themes included gold work, flowers and people. In general, however, the most common themes over the past 100 years, in order of most prevalent to least prevalent, are flowers, especially, roses; fruit, including grapes and berries; game birds, fish and shellfish; human figures and portraits; and, finally, scenes and animals. Likewise, the tastes of collectors have changed over time. Currently, decorative objects with Victorian dressed figures are highly popular with collectors. Hunting objects, such as game birds, game animals and fish are less popular, partly as a result of society's emphasis on animal rights. If viewed in the context of the time they were painted, however, many of the game pieces represent some of the most exquisite examples of the decorative art of Limoges porcelain.

DECORATING METHOD AND STYLE

Decorating method is also an important factor in determining value. Completely hand-painted pieces are, in many instances, more desirable than pieces that are decorated with transfers or pieces that are predominately transfers with hand-painted highlights. Nearly all of the decorative art objects are entirely hand-painted. The signature of an artist, which is usually in the painting, also adds to the value. Some collectors seek out only pieces by such well known Limoges porcelain artists as Renè, Dubois, Luc, L. E. Pic, and Ted Alfred Broussillon. Many of these hand-painted pieces originated as blanks which were stenciled with outlines (transfers) of the subject at the porcelain factories before being painted by hand.

The majority of dinnerware is decorated with transfers, since transfers are applied under the glaze and therefore more durable. A large number of the older dinnerware sets, though, are hand-painted with gold accents. Since many copies were made for a specific event, most of the commemorative pieces were also decorated with transfers. Hand-painted items are not in and of themselves more valuable, however. There are many entirely hand-painted items, even by well known Limoges artists, that are done poorly; while there are many beautiful pieces that are decorated solely with transfers or a combination of transfers and hand-painting.

The trademarks of the non-Haviland Limoges decorative style are hand-painted pieces in deep and vivid colors with heavily gilded accents. The decorative pieces, which are particularly highly sought after, are those with thick gold borders on plates and plaques and gold painted handles, rims and bases on vases, cachepots and jardinieres. The art nouveau style was popular from the late 1880s to the very early 1900s, while the art deco style began in the early 1900s and then was further popularized by the 1925 Paris exhibition, *Arts Décoratifs*.

DECORATING ORIGIN

A lot of attention has been paid to the decorating origin of Limoges porcelain. Some Limoges companies were only decorating studios, others only manufacturers, still others only exporters while some were all three. Often, however, a company started out in just one of the above three areas and then later expanded to include additional functions in either the manufacturing or decorating process.

Much of the very early Limoges porcelain was not marked, either to identify the manufacturer or the decorating studio. For example, President and Mrs. Lincoln, in 1861 and the first to have Haviland Limoges porcelain in the White House, had dinnerware that was unmarked. Even when the manufacturers began to routinely mark their porcelain, beginning in 1891 when the McKinley Tariff Law in the U.S. required imports to indicate the country of origin, the decorating company was not always indicated by a mark. (In 1914 the tariff law was expanded to require the words *made in*.) In fact, after 1891 many of the decorating studios still included only the word *Limoges* and not *France*; and even after 1914, few of the Limoges manufacturers and decorators included the words *made in*. There are many pieces of early Limoges porcelain that were clearly professionally decorated in France, yet bear no decorating mark. Also, a large number of Limoges blanks were decorated in the U.S. by professional decorating studios, such as Pickard and Stouffer, and by professional artists and well as amateurs.

So where does all this leave the collector? Our opinion is that each piece should be judged by its own artistic merit, regardless of the source of decoration, at least in terms of assigning values. Certainly knowing the decorating origin allows us to trace the tastes and styles popular over time in both the U.S. and France and knowing the decorating origin tells us about particular artists and particular companies. Also, many collectors specialize in pieces only decorated in France. In determining values for old Limoges porcelain for this book, however, we have given less emphasis to decorating origin than to artistic merit. Not only does this confirm our own approach to collecting Limoges porcelain, but it also represents what we see occurring in the collector marketplace—at numerous auctions and in conversations with numerous collectors.

AGE OF PORCELAIN

Since we have included photographs of porcelain made over the past 100 plus years, it is important that we talk about age as an element in determining values. Some collectors, for example, only collect 18th century porcelain, others only 19th century porcelain and still others only porcelain that is 100 years old or more—true antiques. Since the first piece of hard-paste Limoges porcelain dates from 1771 and since pieces from the first 75 years are mostly in museums, the great majority of collectors concentrate on pieces dating from 1860s onward. There are still pieces available on the market which date from the second half of the 19th century, but there are, as expected, even more pieces available from the early part of the 20th century. These later pieces tend to be more lavishly decorated. All things being equal, though, the older the porcelain the more highly it is valued, since older pieces are much scarcer. With increasing age, porcelain tends to get chipped and cracked and the paint from the decoration, if it is over the glaze, begins to show wear—all of which tend to decrease somewhat the value of the piece. Most collectors are willing to tolerate some deterioration from wear, such as fading and some disappearance of paint, especially gold decoration, through frequent handling; but most collectors do not want pieces that are chipped and cracked. Only for very old pieces will collectors pay premium prices for porcelain that is physically damaged. At this age pieces will be highly valued because they are so scarce.

SCARCITY AND CONDITION

Relative scarcity also becomes a factor in determining values of pieces that represent blanks that are unusual and that were produced in relatively small numbers. Many of the larger pieces of Limoges porcelain fall into this category. Relatively scarce blanks include, for example, jardinieres, vases with unusual shapes and handles, large chargers and cachepots, glove boxes from dresser sets, large oval plaques with intricately shaped borders, letter boxes, chamber pots with water pitchers and basins, etc. Additionally, there are several Limoges companies that produced a relatively small amount of porcelain or decorated relatively few pieces, and companies that did not have a large export business to the U.S. Pieces from all of these companies tend to command higher prices because few of their works are in circulation. Examples of companies falling into these categories include S. Maas, Oscar Gutherz, François Alluaud, Henri Ardant, and Barny & Rigoni.

QUALITY OF DECORATION

One of the most difficult areas to define is artistic value and quality of decoration. As we stated previously, because a piece is decorated in France does not mean it is well executed. Nor for that matter does a piece decorated by a professional U.S. decorating studio mean it is well done. On balance, however, there are more poorly decorated pieces by amateur U.S. painters than poorly decorated pieces done by professional artists and studios in France and the U.S. What we, as collectors, look for first are pieces that are entirely hand-painted, since many of these pieces have variability and nuances of color, shading and design that are not found in pieces that are decorated with transfers. We are also partial to pieces that have the Limoges trademark of heavily gilded borders and accents, although it is important that the gold accents contribute to the theme of the painting and not detract from it. In some cases, pieces are so heavily gilded that they diminish the subject being depicted. We also look for pieces where the painting acknowledges in some way the specific details of the blank itself; where, for example, ridges and designs in the porcelain are incorporated into the painting and design. For example, if a particular blank has scalloped ridges around the border, we like the painting to acknowledge or incorporate the ridges into the

overall design of the decoration.

In painted pieces with people, we look for individuals attired in clothing of the period with features that are well proportioned and with facial expressions that convey a feeling or mood. It is also important that the background in some sense support the image of the individual or individuals and that both fit the shape of the particular piece of porcelain. In some instances, for example, the figure is off center on the blank or the figure is proportionately too small for the size of the blank. In other cases, the bodies of some figures or their arms or legs look misshapen. In pieces involving more than one individual, we look for some interaction between the individuals, either in terms of their expression or activity. In some of the paintings, the emotions being expressed between two people are very real or they are meaningfully engaged in some joint activity. In pieces of singular individuals, we look for emotions and mood. For example, in a painting by Luc, there is a lone woman fisherman standing by the seashore with a background showing fishing boats out at sea. This woman's connection to her fellow fishermen in the boats and their common but contented way of life is all suggested by her clothing, her holding of a sail and her waving to someone not depicted in the painting. In contrast, there are two brightly costumed cavalier portraits, each of which exhibit different characteristics of a cavalier—one who is jovial with a hint of mischief and the other who is aloof and somewhat arrogant.

As with paintings of people, we expect paintings of animals, birds and fish that are intended to be lifelike to be well proportioned. When there are multiple birds set in a scene, for example, the painting should have depth, where birds and objects in the foreground look closer and are larger than those in the background. The setting is also important. Some settings are quite detailed, containing water, buildings, flowers and other objects. Many of the pieces for serving fish and seafood are elaborately decorated and quite stunning, where the artist has used an abundance of bright colors with heavy use of gold for accents, while still maintaining a sense of the reality of the subject. Other artists give us a simultaneous view of life both above and beneath the water, with, for example, shellfish inhabiting the water's depths and fish breaking through the surface of the water to catch a fly and revealing life on land and in the air. Although many of the game birds are predominately brownish in tone, some have feathers that appear almost textured and some have contrasting colors and backgrounds. Paintings of mallard ducks and pheasants allow the artist to incorporate the naturally bright colors of these species of birds. In other cases, brown game birds may be offset with contrasting and unusual landscapes, such as white snow, lakes and buildings. In some of the paintings, the birds appear to be actually alive and ready to move off the porcelain at the slightest sense of danger; in others, the birds appear to be actually flying or moving. Movement and the sense of danger or heightened awareness are also depicted in paintings of other animals as well.

One of the other major decorating themes of Limoges porcelain is flowers. The majority of the dinnerware sets are decorated with floral transfers and gold highlights. Although most of the dinnerware patterns are floral transfers in subdued colors, often with gold accents, others are brightly colored with lavish use of gold borders and accents. Flowers are also the predominant themes on dresser sets. While decorative pieces have more varied subjects, floral designs also make up a large proportion of these items as well. With decorative pieces, the flowers are more often boldly painted in bright colors, with lavish use of gilt. The more striking paintings are those where the flowers appear fresh and lifelike. With jardinieres, cachepots and vases, the floral theme should encompass the entire piece, and not just one angle or view. In some of the more well executed pieces, the floral design may show some progression as it wraps around a vase or jardiniere; where, for example, sprigs of flowers may be in different stages of opening or where a variety of colors are contrasted and fused. There are also some unusual plate paintings, where floral patterns are used as foregrounds to frame background scenes, giving the piece a sense of depth and dimension. Some painters, using pastels and soft colors, have been able to give floral patterns a wispy effect, where the flowers and foliage are almost floating on the porcelain. While there is an almost limitless number of floral designs, patterns and effects, those we have described are what appeal to us as collectors and which show skill and thought on the part of the painter.

We need to point out that there are many other decorative themes included on Limoges porcelain. Popular subjects also include different fruits, with grapes being especially popular with American painters; cherubs; patterns reflecting Oriental influences; art deco designs; and interesting abstract uses of shapes and colors.

Finally, there are some entirely hand-painted pieces which appear to be transfers, because the painting is so precise and repeated patterns are nearly identical in shape and color. Many of these pieces are superbly executed reproductions of 17th and 18th century porcelain pieces that are now in museums. There are only a few decorating studios that currently make these fine reproductions.

Summary

There are a number of factors affecting the value and desirability of any piece of Limoges porcelain. Different collectors, depending upon their objectives and tastes, will place different values on each of these factors. The general popularity of particular themes also changes over time.

At the end of the 20th century, a highly desirable piece of Limoges porcelain would be described as follows: It would be a large, hand-painted vase, 12 or more inches tall, with full length figures of Victorian dressed women on two sides. It would carry the signature of an artist who could be either French or American; and the handles, rim and base would be heavily gilded. The vase would have no chips, cracks or signs of wear; and it would have been painted prior to 1920.

In the 21st century, the highly desirable piece of Limoges porcelain will surely be described differently, reflecting the changes in tastes and attitudes of collectors and society in general. The term, "highly desirable," fortunately, only has meaning when establishing values, since increased demand for certain kinds of items is reflected in increased prices. Thankfully, there are many beautiful pieces of older Limoges porcelain in a wide range of subject matters and decorating styles. So for collectors who have eclectic tastes and a broad appreciation of beauty, they will not have to be concerned with what is popular at the moment.

Photographs of Limoges Porcelain

The photographs for Limoges porcelain, excluding the Limoges boxes, are divided into four main sections. The first grouping includes chargers, plaques and distinctive plates. Since many of these items are primarily decorative pieces, many of them are hand-painted. In some cases, we included plates in this section instead of the section on dinnerware, since the decoration or the blank was in some way distinctive.

The second section includes mostly vases and jardinieres. Like the items in the first section, the pieces here are also primarily decorative and therefore hand-painted. While decorative vases represent many different subjects, the majority of jardinieres and cachepots have floral themes. In both the first and second sections, we have grouped together similar subjects, which will give the reader the opportunity to compare various decorating techniques, the styles of different artists, the varieties of porcelain blanks and changes in taste over time.

The third section brings together many unusual—and some not so unusual—specialty items. It includes, for example, such pieces as figurines, buttons, decanters, lamps and dresser items. This section will give the reader some notion of the variety of different items that were made by the Limoges porcelain companies.

The last section includes many specialty serving items. Instead of emphasizing dinnerware and the multitude of different china patterns, we have chosen instead to include special-purpose pieces, many of which are highly decorated and often hand-painted . These include, among other things, tea; chocolate and coffee sets; punch bowls and tankards.

Where there are two or more marks for an item, the first mark is the decorating mark.

Chargers, Plaques and Distinctive Plates

Charger, 15.25" in diameter. Klingenberg, mark 4; artist, Dubois. $800-$1,200.

Charger, 16" in diameter. Tressemanes & Vogt, mark 10; artist, M.B.H. '09. $800-$1,200.

Plaque, 13.25" high x 9.25" wide, rare blank.
Coiffe, mark 3; artist, Greer. $800-$1,000.

Charger, 13" in diameter. Lazarus Straus &
Sons, mark 1; artist, Dubois. $600-$800.

Charger, 15.5" in diameter. Lazeyras, Rosenfeld & Lehman;
artist, Dubois. *Courtesy of Bruce Guilmette.* $1,000-$1,400.

Charger, 15.75" in diameter.
Délinières, mark 2. $400-$500.

Plaque, 5.75" high x 7.75" wide. Tressemanes & Vogt, mark 10; artist, FMM. $300-$400.

Plaque, 14" high x 7" wide, rare blank. Tressemanes & Vogt, mark 10. *Courtesy of Jacqueline Lowensteiner*. $1,000-$1,200.

Above: Charger, 13.5" in diameter. Lazeyras, Rosenfeld & Lehman, mark 1 and Limoges, mark 5; artist, Buzanay or Bzaranay, signature unclear. *Courtesy of Jacqueline Lowensteiner*. $600-$1,000.

Right: Plate, 10" in diameter. Lazeyras, Rosenfeld & Lehman, mark 3; artist, Gilbot. *Courtesy of Jacqueline Lowensteiner*. $400-$600.

Above left: Plate, 10" in diameter. T. Haviland, mark L; artist, L. Jean. *Courtesy of Yasumasa Tanano.* $275-$325.

Above right: Plate, 10" in diameter. T. Haviland, mark L; artist, L. Jean. *Courtesy of Yasumasa Tanano.* $275-$325.

Left: Plate, 10" in diameter. T. Haviland, mark L; artist, L. Jean. *Courtesy of Yasumasa Tanano.* $275-$325.

Plaque, 7" high x 4.5" wide. Tharaud, mark 2. $200-$300.

Plate, 6.4" in diameter. T. Haviland, mark P. $75-$85.

Plate, 10.5" in diameter. Borgfeldt, mark 1 and Limoges, mark 3; artist, Dubois. *Courtesy of Jacqueline Lowensteiner.* $400-$600.

Plate, 9.5" in diameter. Bawo & Dotter, mark 4 and Limoges, mark 1. $125-$175.

Plate, 9.9" in diameter. Borgfeldt, mark 1; artist, Luc. $150-$225.

Plate, 7" square. Gérard, Dufraisseix, marks 2 and 1.
Courtesy of Yasumasa Tanano. $125-$175.

Plate, 10" in diameter. Lazeyras, Rosenfeld & Lehman, mark 1; artist, J. Mongars. *Courtesy of Jacqueline Lowensteiner.* $400-$600.

Platter, 8.5" high x 10.5" wide. Haviland & Co., mark H; artist, M.E. Farrier 98. *Courtesy of Jacqueline Lowensteiner.* $150-$175.

Above: Plaque, 9" high x 6.75" wide. Délinières, mark 2; artist, Henrietta Curtis 1921. $250-$350.

Right: Charger, 13.25" in diameter. Borgfeldt, mark 1; artist, Armond. $400-$600.

Plate, 8.5" in diameter. Bawo & Dotter,
mark 4 and Coiffe, mark 2. $75-$100.

Plate, 7" square. Pouyat, mark 3. $50-$75.

Plate, 9.5" in diameter. Marked 1978 by Haviland
for Franklin; artist signature illegible. $25-$30.

Plate, 9.5" in diameter. Tressemanes & Vogt,
marks 12 and 8. $100-$125.

Plate, 8" square. Gérard, Dufraisseix & Morel, mark 1.
Courtesy of Yasumasa Tanano. $300+.

Plate, 8" square. Gérard, Dufraisseix & Morel, mark 1.
Courtesy of Yasumasa Tanano. $300+.

Plate, 8" square. Gérard, Dufraisseix & Morel, mark 1.
Courtesy of Yasumasa Tanano. $300+.

Plate, 8" square. Gérard, Dufraisseix & Morel, mark 1.
Courtesy of Yasumasa Tanano. $300+.

Plate, 7.5" in diameter. Haviland & Co., marks g and D; also marked: Home again; artist, Kate Greenaway. *Courtesy of Yasumasa Tanano.* $150-$200.

Plate, 7.5" in diameter. Haviland & Co., marks g and D; also marked: Four hours after, "Patience is a virtue etc"; artist, Kate Greenaway. *Courtesy of Yasumasa Tanano.* $150-$200.

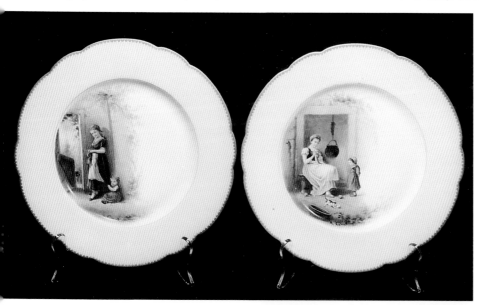

Left & below: Plates, 8.5" in diameter. Haviland & Co., mark D; artist, A. Collot. *Courtesy of Tom Roth.* Set of twelve plates, $3,000+.

Plate, 10" in diameter. Borgfeldt,
mark 1; artist, Luc. *Courtesy of
Jacqueline Lowensteiner.* $150-250.

Plate, 9" in diameter. T. Haviland, mark q; artist, J. Martin.
Courtesy of Yasumasa Tanano. $100-$125.

Plate, 10" in diameter. Borgfeldt, mark
1; artist, L.E. Pic. *Courtesy of Jacqueline
Lowensteiner.* $150-$250.

Plate, 10" in diameter. Borgfeldt,
mark 1; artist, Luc. $150-$250.

Plate, 10.6" in diameter. Borgfeldt, mark 1 and Mavaleix, mark 1; artist, L. Coudert. *Courtesy of Jacqueline Lowensteiner.* $150-$250.

Plate, 10.6" in diameter. Borgfeldt, mark 1 and Mavaleix, mark 1; artist, L. Coudert. $150-$250.

Plate, 10.6" in diameter. Borgfeldt, mark 1 and Mavaleix, mark 1; artist, L. Coudert. $150-$250.

Plate, 9" in diameter. Lazeyras, Rosenfeld & Lehman, mark 3 and Limoges, mark 7; artist, S. Soustre. *Courtesy of Jacqueline Lowensteiner.* $300-$500.

Charger, 13" in diameter. Tressemanes & Vogt, mark 10.
Courtesy of Jacqueline Lowensteiner. $800-$1,200.

Plaque, 5" in diameter, McKinley mourning portrait
and frame, 1901. Guérin, mark 4. $225-$300.

Plate, 9.6" in diameter. Haviland & Co., mark I; marked
Duchess of Kent; artist, Mabel E. Howard '06. $100-$125.

Plate, 9.6" in diameter. Haviland & Co., mark I; marked
Queen Louisa; artist, Mabel E. Howard '06. $100-$125.

Plate, 10" in diameter, rare Indian subject.
Blakeman & Henderson, mark 2; marked
Chief Wets-it, Assinniboine. $200-$300.

Plate, 8.5" in diameter. Pouyat, mark 7;
artist, Millie G. Porter 1893. $100-$125.

Plate, 8.5" in diameter, Pouyat, mark 3; artist,
Millie G. Porter 1893. $100-$125.

Set of Eight Fairy Plates, 7.25" in diameter.
Haviland & Co., mark F. $400-$500 for set.

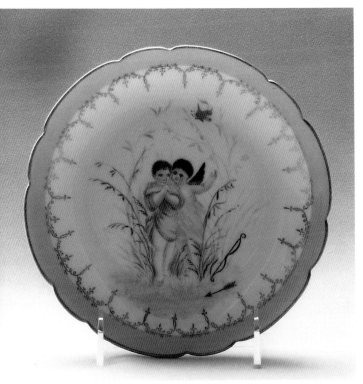

Tray, 8" high x 11" wide. Tressemanes
& Vogt, Mark 10. $125-$175.

Plate, 9.9" in diameter. Borgfeldt,
mark 1; artist. L.E. Pic. $100-$125.

Plate, 11.25" in diameter. Lazarus Straus & Sons,
mark 1 and Limoges, mark 3. $350-$400.

Plate, 9.25" in diameter. Tressemanes
& Vogt, mark 8. $75-100.

One Platter and Twelve Plates in Twelve Days of Christmas Series, 12.4" in diameter for platter and 8.5" in diameter for plates. T. Haviland, mark t; artist, r. hétreau. $500-$600 for set.

1970

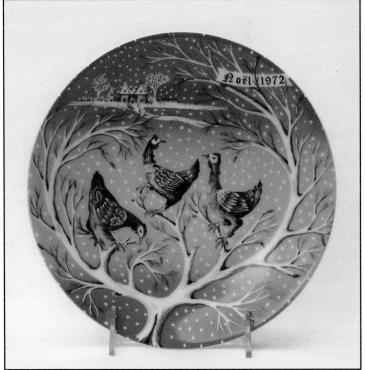

1971

1972

1973

1974

1975

1976

1977

1978

1979

1980

1981

Three Plates, 7" high x 6.75" wide. Gutherz,
mark 2 and impressed, 83. $300 for set.

Charger, 13.4" in diameter. Flambeau, mark 5; artist, signature illegible. $450-$650.

Plate, 8.75" in diameter. Borgfeldt, mark 2 and Coiffe, mark 3. $30-$50.

Above: Plate, 10" in diameter. Bawo & Dotter, marks 10 and 11; artist, E. Vidal. *Courtesy of Jacqueline Lowensteiner.* $250-$350.

Right: Tray, 12.5" high x 15" wide. Barny & Rigoni, mark 1. *Courtesy of Jacqueline Lowensteiner.* $300-$400.

Six Plates, 6" in diameter. Bawo &
Dotter, mark 11; artist, FF. $150-$175

Plate, 10" in diameter, unusual subject.
Paroutaud, mark 1. $100-$125.

Charger, 12" in diameter. Lazeyras, Rosenfeld &
Lehman, mark 3 and Legrand, mark 1; artist,
Buzanay or Bzaranay, signature unclear. *Courtesy
of Jacqueline Lowensteiner.* $175-$225.

Charger, 13.5" in diameter, unusual blank. Lazarus Straus & Sons, mark 1; artist, signature illegible. *Courtesy of Jacqueline Lowensteiner.* $250-$300.

Charger, 13.5" in diameter. R. Haviland, mark 1; artist, Marcadet. *Courtesy of Jacqueline Lowensteiner.* $400-$550.

Charger, 13" in diameter. Lazarus Straus & Sons, mark 1; artist, Dubois. $400-$550.

Charger, 13" in diameter. Lazarus Straus & Sons, mark 1; artist, Dubois. $400-550.

Charger, 13" in diameter. Limoges, mark 12; artist, Dubois. $400-$550.

Charger, 13" in diameter. Lazarus Straus & Sons, mark 1; artist, Dubois. $400-$550.

Charger, 13" in diameter. C. et J., mark 1; artist, Ted Alfred Broussillon, $400-$550.

Plate, 10" in diameter. Lazeyras, Rosenfeld & Lehman, mark 3; artist, Henkies, signature unclear. $75-$125.

Plate, 10" in diameter. Borgfeldt, mark 1; artist, Dulac. *Courtesy of Jacqueline Lowensteiner.* $125-$150.

Three Plates, 9.5" in diameter. Raynaud, mark 7 and Limoges, mark 1; artist, Depitour. $200-$250 for set.

Charger, 13" in diameter, unusual blank. Blakeman & Henderson, mark 2; artist, Dulac. *Courtesy of Jacqueline Lowensteiner.* $450-600.

Plate, 8.5" in diameter. Pouyat, marks 4 and 3. $100-$150.

Plate, 10.25" in diameter. Borgfeldt, mark 1; artist, Dubois. $125-$150.

Plate, 10" in diameter. Blakeman & Henderson, mark 2. $75-$125.

Plate, 10"
in diameter.
Borgfeldt,
mark 1; artist,
Dulac.
*Courtesy of
Jacqueline
Lowensteiner.*
$125-$150.

Above: Plate, 9.75" in diameter. Lazeyras, Rosenfeld & Lehman, mark 2; artist, Dubois. $125-$150.

Right: Plate, 10" in diameter. Flambeau, marks 3 and 1; artist, Dubois. $125-$150.

Above: Charger, 16" in diameter. Lazeyras, Rosenfeld & Lehman, mark 2; artist, Dubois. *Courtesy of Jacqueline Lowensteiner.* $800-$1,000.

Right: Charger, 14" in diameter. Blakeman & Henderson, mark 2 and Limoges, mark 3; artist, J. Morray. *Courtesy of Jacqueline Lowensteiner.* $450-$600.

Plate, 10.75" in diameter. Mavaleix,
mark 1; artist, L. Coudert. $75-$125.

Plate, 10.25" in diameter. Borgfeldt,
mark 1; artist, Luc. $125-$150.

Plate, 10.25" in diameter. Blakeman & Henderson,
mark 2 and Limoges, mark 6. $75-$100.

Plate, 10" in diameter. Flambeau,
marks 4 and 1. $65-$95.

Plate, 10" in diameter. Flambeau, marks
5 and 1; artist, Dubois. $125-$150.

Plate. 9.25" in diameter. Barny & Rigoni,
mark 4 and Coiffe, mark 2. $75-$125.

Charger, 12.5"
in diameter.
Haviland & Co.,
mark h; artist, E.
Lainy, signature
unclear. *Courtesy
of Jacqueline
Lowensteiner.*
$500-$700.

Above: Plate, 9.25" in diameter. Lazarus Straus &
Sons, mark 1 and Coiffe, mark 2. $50-$75.

Right: Charger, 13" in diameter. Lazeyras,
Rosenfeld & Lehman, mark 1; artist, Dubois.
Courtesy of Jacqueline Lowensteiner. $300-$375.

Plate, 11.5" in diameter. Borgfeldt, mark 1; artist, Duval. *Courtesy of Jacqueline Lowensteiner.* $300-$350.

Charger, 13" in diameter. Flambeau, mark 4; artist, signature illegible. $300-$400.

Tray, 16" wide. Tressemanes & Vogt, mark 11; artist, E. R. Fuller. *Courtesy of Bruce Guilmette.* $300-$400.

Charger, 16" in diameter. Borgfeldt, mark 1; artist, A. Baunnelly. *Courtesy of Bruce Guilmette.* $800-$1,000.

Charger, 12.5" in diameter. Blakeman & Henderson, mark 1; artist, J. Morsey. *Courtesy of Dorla I. Battersby.* $300-$400.

Charger, 13" in diameter. Borgfeldt, mark 1; artist, Duval. *Courtesy of Jacqueline Lowensteiner.* $400-$500.

Two Plates, 8.25" in diameter. Ahrenfeldt, mark 1. $150-$200 for set.

Plate, 10.25" in diameter. Strawbridge & Clothier, mark 1. *Courtesy of Bruce Guilmette*. $150-$175.

Charger, 12" in diameter. Lanternier, mark 5. *Courtesy of Bruce Guilmette*. $150-$200.

Plate, 10.75" in diameter. Blakeman & Henderson, mark 2 and Coiffe, mark 3; artist, Y. Mcoiscic. *Courtesy of Bruce Guilmette*. $125-$175.

Charger, 16" in diameter. Flambeau, mark 2 and Limoges, mark 3. *Courtesy of Bruce Guilmette*. $800-$1,000.

Plaque, 13.25" high x 9.25" wide, rare blank. Coiffe, mark 3. *Courtesy of Bruce Guilmette*. $700+.

Charger, 12.25" in diameter. Pouyat, mark 7; artist, M. M^{c}M. *Courtesy of Bruce Guilmette*. $200-$250.

Charger, 12" in diameter. Bower & Dotter, marks 10 and 11; artist, Gilbot. *Courtesy of Jacqueline Lowensteiner*. $250-$300.

Plate, 9.5" in diameter. Flambeau, mark 3 and Limoges, mark 1; artist, Moch, Koch or Roch, signature unclear. $100-$125.

Charger, 13" in diameter. Levy, mark 1; artist, Jubal. *Courtesy of Bruce Guilmette.* $550+.

Charger, 12" in diameter. Tressemanes & Vogt, mark 9. *Courtesy of Bruce Guilmette.* $200-$300.

Charger, 12.25" in diameter, unusual blank. Lazarus Straus & Sons, mark 1 and Limoges, mark 7. $150-$200.

Tray, 17.5" in diameter. Gérard, Dufraisseix, Abbot, mark 6. *Courtesy of Bruce Guilmette.* $400-$500.

Top left: Charger, 16" in diameter. Tressemanes & Vogt, mark 10; artist, M. Comeford. *Courtesy of Bruce Guilmette.* $450-$600.

Top right: Charger, 14" in diameter. Klingenberg, mark 8. *Courtesy of Bruce Guilmette.* $500+.

Center left: Charger, 12" in diameter. Flambeau, mark 3 and Limoges, mark 3; artist, Marc. $150-$200.

Center right: Plaque, 13.5" wide, rare blank. Coiffe, mark 3. *Courtesy of Bruce Guilmette.* $300+.

Left: Charger, 13" in diameter. A&D, mark 1; artist, Ted Alfred Broussillon. *Courtesy of Bruce Guilmette.* $600+.

Charger, 12" in diameter. Klingenberg, mark 9; artist, L.M.A. *Courtesy of Bruce Guilmette.* $300+.

Plate, 8.5" in diameter. Tressemanes & Vogt, mark 13. *Courtesy of Dorla I. Battersby.* $150-$250.

Plate, 11" in diameter, unusual blank. Plaine Maison, mark 1. *Courtesy of Bruce Guilmette.* $250+.

Charger, 12.75" in diameter. Pouyat, mark 7. *Courtesy of Bruce Guilmette.* $350+.

Four Plates, 10.75" in diameter. Guérin, marks 6
and 4; artist, Mary Bacon Jones. $1,000+ for set.

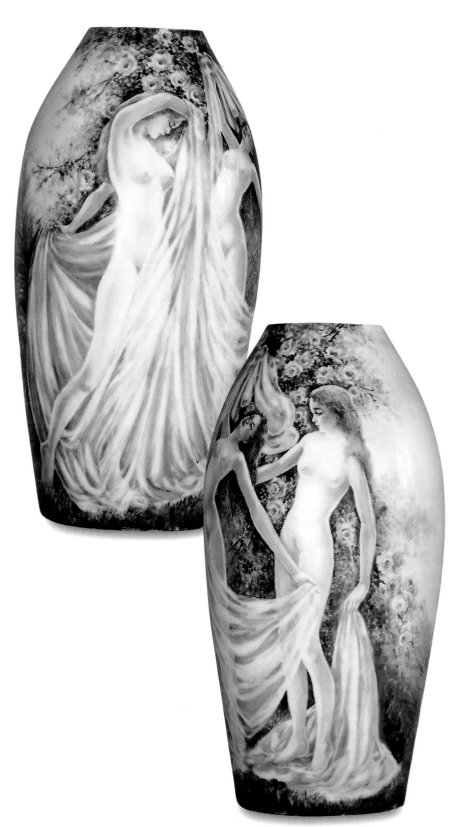

Three Sides of Vase, 13"
high. Other, mark 1. artist,
Cummins. $1,000-$1,200.

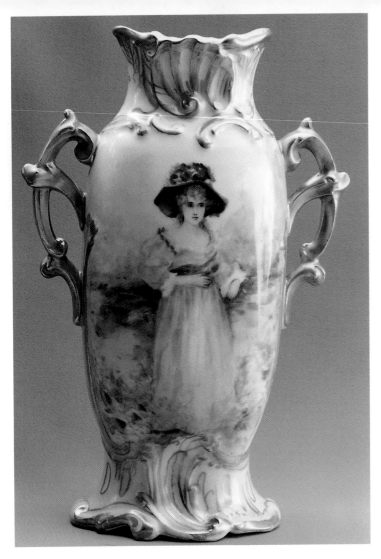

Above two: Two Sides of Vase, 11" high. Bawo & Dotter, mark 4. $700+.

Left: Vase, 10.1" high. Bawo & Dotter, mark 4. $500-$600.

Two Sides of Vase, 13.25" high. Lazeyras,
Rosenfeld & Lehman, mark 1. $400+.

Three Sides of Vase, 22.25" high. Tressemanes &
Vogt, mark 10; artist, L. Geagren. $1,800-$2,200.

Far left: Vase. 14.25" high. Tressemanes & Vogt, mark 10; artist, Steiner, possibly a Pickard artist. $700-$850.

Above: Vase, 4" high. Délinières, mark 2; artist, ELM. $150-$200.

Left: Vase, 5.75" high, unusual subject. Tressemanes & Vogt, mark 10; marked Jul. H. Brauer, Hand Painted China (a professional decorating company). $150-$200.

Two at right: Two Sides of Vase, 18" high. Bawo & Dotter, marks 4 and 11. *Courtesy of Bruce Guilmette.* $1,400+.

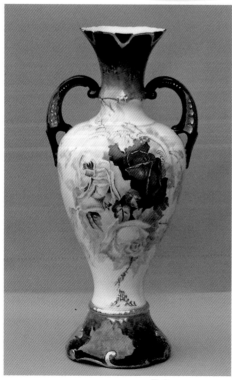

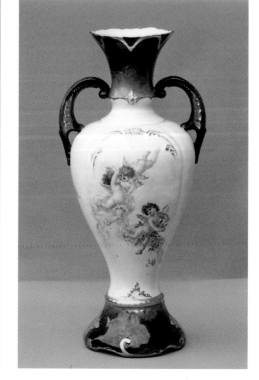

Above: Vase, 28" high. Guérin, mark 4. *Courtesy of Bruce Guilmette.* $1,500+.

Right: Vase, 16.25" high. Guérin, mark 4. *Courtesy of Bruce Guilmette.* $500-$700.

Above: Vase, 11.5" high. Pouyat, mark 7. $500-$600.

Right: Vase, 4.25" high. Tressemanes & Vogt, mark 10; artist, H. Chambers. *Courtesy of Dorla I. Battersby.* $175-$250.

Vase, 10.5" high. Pouyat, mark 7; artist, E.M. Penne.
Courtesy of Bruce Guilmette. $675+.

Basket Vase, 7" high. Mavaleix,
mark 1. $100-$125.

Vase, 6.5" high. Délinières, mark 2; artist, A.F. Baldwin.
Courtesy of Bruce Guilmette. $225+.

Vase, 12.75" high, unusual shaped handles.
Latrille, mark 1; artist, M. Mackenzie. *Courtesy
of Bruce Guilmette.* $400-$600.

Vase, 14.5" high. Tressemanes & Vogt, mark 10; artist, A.E. Williams. *Courtesy of Bruce Guilmette*. $300-$500.

Vase. Pouyat, marks 8 and 7. *Courtesy of Jacqueline Lowensteiner*. $350-$400.

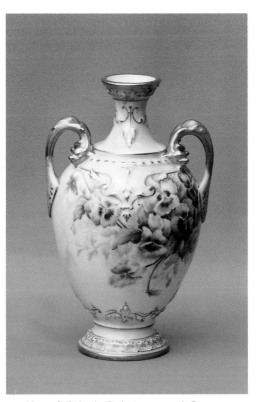

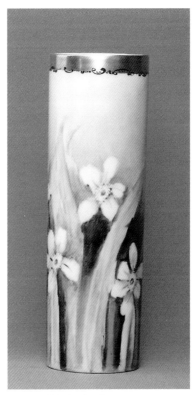

Vase, 9.5" high. Délinières, mark 2. *Courtesy of Bruce Guilmette*. $300+.

Bud Vase, 4.5" high. Délinières, mark 2. *Courtesy of Bruce Guilmette*. $150-$200.

Vase, 9.5" high. Guérin, mark 4. $100-$125.

Vase, 15" high. Bawo & Dotter, mark 4.
Courtesy of Bruce Guilmette. $800+.

Ferner, 3.5" high x 8.5" in diameter. Limoges,
mark 9; artist, P. Colean '07. $100-$125.

Cachepot, 10.5" high. Guérin, mark 4.
Courtesy of Bruce Guilmette. $600+.

Cachepot, 9.75" high. Guérin, mark 4.
Courtesy of Bruce Guilmette. $600+.

Jardiniere, with Lion Heads, 11.25" high x 14.5" at handles. Délinières, mark 2. $800-$1,200.

Lion head handle of jardiniere.

Above: Jardiniere, 10.75" high. Délinières, mark 2. *Courtesy of Bruce Guilmette.* $1,100+.

Left: Jardiniere, 8.75" high. Délinières, mark 2. *Courtesy of Bruce Guilmette.* $500+.

Jardiniere, with Elephant Heads, 8.5" high. Pouyat, mark 7; artist, S.R. Meck 1896. *Courtesy of Bruce Guilmette.* $800+.

Jardiniere, 9" high. Tressemanes & Vogt, mark 8. *Courtesy of Bruce Guilmette.* $400-$600.

Jardiniere, 10.5" high. Délinières, mark 2. *Courtesy of Bruce Guilmette.* $900-$1,300.

Jardiniere, with Lion Heads, 11.25" high. Délinières, mark 2. *Courtesy of Bruce Guilmette.* $800-$1,200.

Right: Planter, 10" high. Guérin, mark 4. *Courtesy of Bruce Guilmette.* $300-$400.

Below: Jardiniere, with Elephant Heads, 7.5" high. Pouyat, mark 7; artist, KWJ 1893. *Courtesy of Bruce Guilmette.* $800+.

Planter, 11.5" high. Stand, Pouyat, mark 7; planter, Guérin, mark 2; artist, Fanny H. Kilbourne. *Courtesy of Bruce Guilmette.* $400-$600.

Above: Jardiniere, 7.5" high. Stand, Limoges, mark 1; jardiniere, Klingenberg, mark 9. *Courtesy of Bruce Guilmette.* $600+.

Left: Jardiniere, with Elephant Heads, 11.5" high. Pouyat, mark 7. *Courtesy of Bruce Guilmette.* $800-$1,200.

Specialty Items

Mephistopheles Humidor, 8" high, *extremely rare.*
Haviland & Co., mark A impressed (1855). $8,000+.

Humidor, 5.5" high. Limoges,
mark 3. $75-$125.

Ashtray, 4.75" wide x 2.9" deep.
Limoges, mark 3. $40-$50.

Ashtray. J.B., mark 1, $20-$30.

Matchbox with Striker, 4.25"
wide x 2.25" deep. Guérin,
marks 5 and 2. $75-$125.

Candlesticks,
6.1" high. Le
Tallec, mark 3,
1997. *Courtesy
of Lucy Zahran
& Company*.
$1,850 for pair.

Candlesticks, 5.75" high.
Lanternier, mark 3. $60-$75.

Candlesticks, 5" high. Tressemanes & Vogt, mark 10.
Courtesy of Bruce Guilmette. $75-$100.

Candlesticks, 9.25" high. Guérin, mark 4.
Courtesy of Bruce Guilmette. $150-$200.

Candlestick, 7.75" high. Martin, mark 1; artist, L.
Leonard. *Courtesy of Bruce Guilmette.* $40-$50.

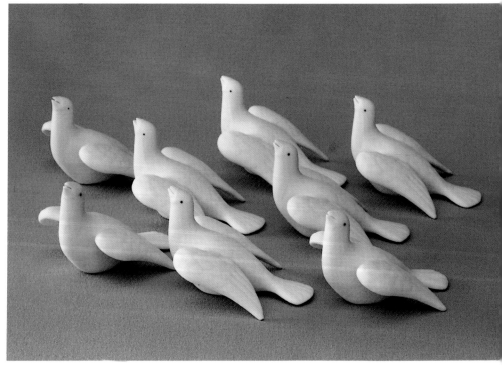

Candlestick, 7.75" high.
Bernardaud, mark 1. $40-$50.

Name Holders, 3.25" x 2.4". Limoges,
mark 1. Set of eight, $100-$200.

Busts, 7.25" high. Manufacture
Nouvelle, mark 1. $100-$125.

Figurine, 7.5" high. T. Haviland, mark p
impressed; artist, L. Savine. $3,000+.

Sculptor's signature.

Figurine, 5" high x 11"
wide. T. Haviland, mark
p impressed and metal
disk with Copyright by
Th. Haviland. *Courtesy
of Tom Roth*. $3,000+.

Lady Figurine, 4.25" high. Limoges Castel, mark 1. $50-$75.

Lady Figurine, 11.5" high. Impressed underglaze, Joe Descomps Limoges and impressed on side Joe Descomps; artist, Joe Descomps. $300-$600.

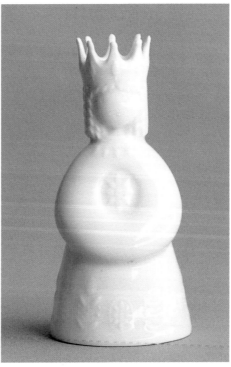

Figurine, 7.5" high. Tharaud, mark 2 and Limoges, mark 1. $75-$100.

Figurine, 5.25" high. T. Haviland, mark R. *Courtesy of Yasumasa Tanano.* $75-$100.

Figurine, 5" high. T. Haviland, mark R. *Courtesy of Yasumasa Tanano.* $75-$100.

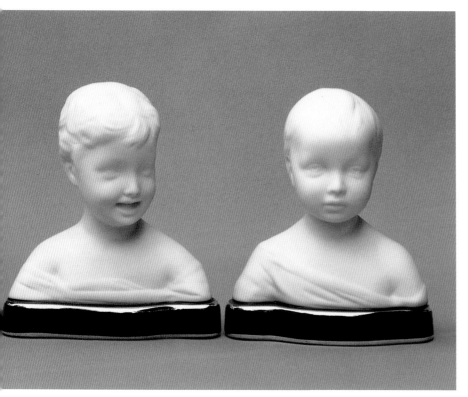

Busts, 5.5" high. Tharaud, mark 2
and Limoges, mark 3. $100-$125.

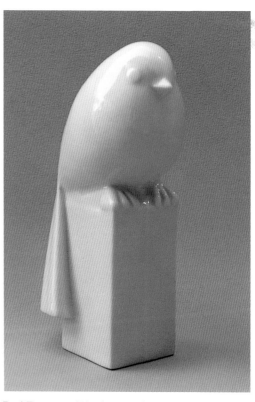

Bird Figurine, 6" high, rare. Gérard,
Dufraisseix, Abbot, mark 6. $300-$400.

Chicken Figurine, 4.5" high. T.
Haviland, mark R. *Courtesy of
Yasumasa Tanano*. $50-$75.

Elephant Figurine, 7" high and 10.5" long. T. Haviland,
similar to mark Q impressed. $300-$500.

Decanter, 10" high. Michelaud, mark 2; marked Robj, Paris. Made in France. $250-$300.

Decanter, 15" high. Limoges, mark 15; marked 13375/15000, D'Apres Original Créé par Jean Mercier en 1936. $50-$75.

Decanter, 4.5" high. Limoges, mark 2; marked P. Garnier. $50-$100.

Decanter, 8.9" high. Bernardaud, marks 6 and 3; marked Bi-Centenaire de L'Empereur Napoléon, 1769-1969. $50-$75.

Decanter, 5.5" high. T. Haviland, mark t; marked Production Réservée: Armagnac Chabot. *Courtesy of Yasumasa Tanano.* $50-$75.

Dessert Fox Bonbon Box, 4.75" high x 7" ear to ear. T. Haviland, marks p and M impressed (1921); artist, E. Sandoz. $800-$1,200.

Parrot Pitcher, 7" high and 9.75" from beak to end of tail. T. Haviland, marks p and M impressed; artist, E. Sandoz. $800-$1,200.

Cat Bonbon Box, 4.6" high. T. Haviland, marks p, M impressed, and O; artist, E. Sandoz. $800-$1,000.

Tea Set: tea pot, 5" high; tray, 10.5" wide x 5" deep; cups, 1.25" high x 2.75" in diameter. T. Haviland, marks p and M impressed for tea pot and tray; marks o, M impressed, and O for cups; artist, E. Sandoz. *Courtesy of Yasumasa Tanano*. $1,200-$1,500 for set.

Cat Pitcher, 7.25" high. T. Haviland, marks p and M impressed; artist, E. Sandoz. *Courtesy of Yasumasa Tanano.* $300-$350.

Frog and Mushroom Salt & Pepper. T. Haviland marks p and M for frog; marks p and O for mushroom. *Courtesy of Yasumasa Tanano.* $350-500 for set.

Figurine Lamp, 9.4" high. Téxeraud, mark 2. $400-$600.

Lamp, 9" high. Porcelaine Limousine, mark 1; artist, Cavin Stun. $100-$125.

Change Trays, 5" in diameter. T. Haviland, marks p and O. $50-$60 each.

Tip Tray, 6" x 3.6" oval. R. Haviland, mark 3. $60-$75.

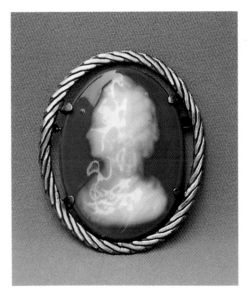

Above: Broach, 2" x 1.4" oval. Tharaud, mark 1. $175-$225.

Left: Pendant, 1.75" x 1.25" oval. Limoges, mark 3; marked Limoges M France in raised letters. $75-$125.

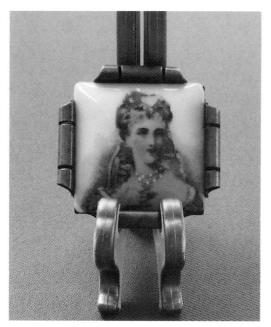

Broach, 1.25" square.
Limoges, mark 3. $75-$100.

Broach, 1.75" x 1.4" oval.
Limoges, mark 3. $30-$50.

Buttons, 0.5" in diameter. G. Boyer,
mark 4. $15-$17 each.

Buttons, 0.9" square. Bawo &
Dotter, mark 4. $35-$45 each.

Doll, 17" high. Lanternier, marked
Fabrication Francaise AL & Cie
Limoges. About 1917. $700-$1200.

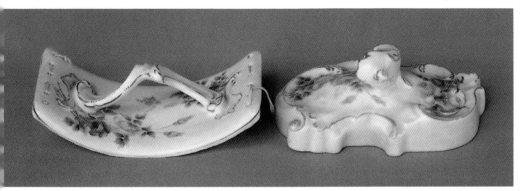

Above: Blotter and Paper Weight; blotter, 5.9" x 3.25"; paper weight, 5.6" x 3.75". Tressemanes & Vogt, mark 10. *Courtesy of Lisa Orr.* $175-$250 for set.

Right: Letter Holder, 6.25" high x 8.4" wide x 3.6" deep. Lanternier, marks 6 and 5. $225-$275.

Below: Picture Frame, 6.75" x 4.75". Klingenberg, mark 8. $75-$125.

Below right: Spit Cup, 3" high x 5" long. Paroutaud, mark 3. $100-$125.

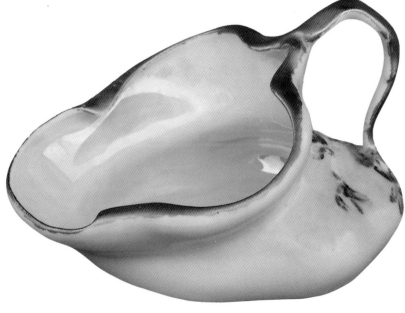

Left: Mug and Covered Soap Dish. Haviland & Co., mark C impressed. *Courtesy of Tom Roth.* $250-$300 for set.

Below: Spit Cup, 3" high x 5" long. Tressemanes & Vogt, mark 10; artist, D. Carey. $100-$125.

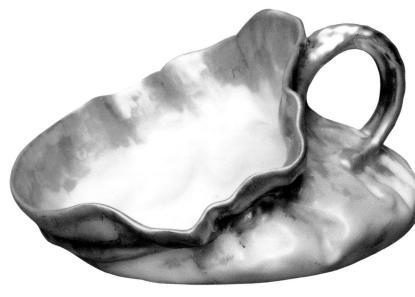

Above: Clock, 10.5" high. Bawo & Dotter, mark 5, extremely rare mark. $500-$800.

Right: Shaving Mug, 4" high x 3.75" in diameter. Haviland & Co., mark g and F. *Courtesy of Yasumasa Tanano.* $100-$150.

Vanity Box, 4.25" high x 14" wide x 8.75" deep. Artoria, mark 4. *Courtesy of Artoria Limoges*. $900-$1,000.

Nine Christmas Ornaments, beginning with 1971. T. Haviland, 1971-1979; artist, Jean Jacques Prolongeau. $180+ for set.

1972

1973

1974

1975

1976. *Courtesy of Yasumasa Tanano.*

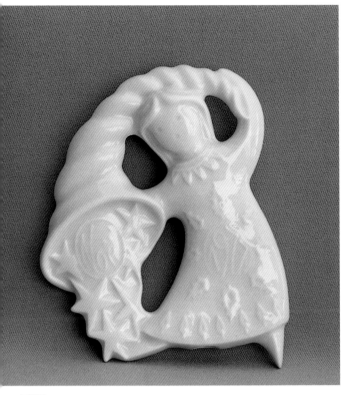

1977

1978

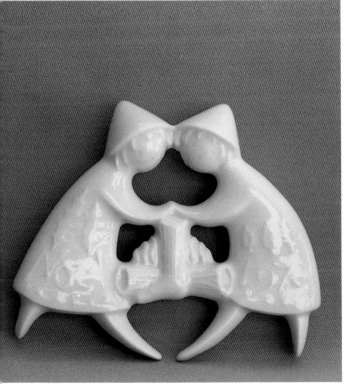

1979

First in a series
of Christmas
Ornaments,
1980. T.
Haviland; artist,
Jacob
Descombes.
$15-$20.

Store Display, 4.75" x 2.5". $55-$65.

Store Display, 2.1" high x 3.5" wide. $40-$50.

Store Display, 3.5" high x 5" wide. Gérard, Dufraisseix, Abbot. $30-$40.

Store Display, 3" high x 5.5" wide. Chamart. $30-$40.

Store Display, 5.75" x 2". $30-$40.

Above: Store Display, 3.75" x 2.6". $40-$50.

Left: Dresser Set, pieces range from 6.75" to 4.4" high. Le Tallec, mark 3, 1950. $2,000+.

Powder Box, 4.75" high. Michelaud, mark 1. $225-$325.

Powder Box, 6.5" high. Michelaud, mark 1. $300-$400.

Dresser Box, 3" high x 5.5" square.
Délinières, marks 4 and 2. $200-$250.

Dresser Box, 2" high x 5" square.
Limoges, mark 3. $125-$150.

Dresser Box, 3.75" high
x 11.6" wide x 4.5"
deep. Délinières, mark
2. $175-$250.

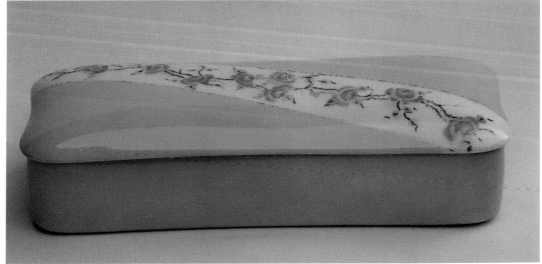

Glove Box, 3" high x
10.5" wide x 3.5"
deep. Plaine Maison,
mark 1. $175-$250.

Dresser Box, 2.75" high x 3.75" in diameter. Maas, mark 1. $125-$150.

Ring Tree, 2.5" high x 3.9" in diameter. Tressemanes & Vogt, marks 12 and 11. $65-$85.

Ring Tree, 3.5" high. Gérard, Dufraisseix & Morel, mark 1. *Courtesy of Yasumasa Tanano.* $65-$85.

Pin Tray, 5.1" long x 3.75" wide. Royal China, mark 1 and Haviland & Co., mark H. $50-$60.

Small Jar, 2.5" high, Délinières, mark 2.
Courtesy of Bruce Guilmette. $50-$60.

Dresser Bottle, 4.4" high. Tressemanes &
Vogt, mark 8.1; artist, Kathryn. $50-$60.

Back of Hand Mirror, 2.75" in diameter.
Limoges, mark 3. $50-$75.

Dresser Tray, 12" wide. Pouyat, mark 7; artist, AGG
1896. *Courtesy of Bruce Guilmette*. $150-$200.

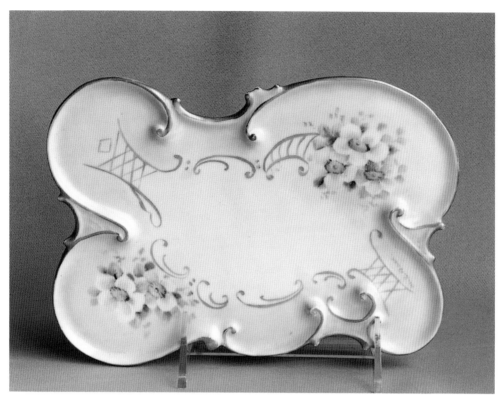

Dresser Tray, 7.5" x 5.25". Gérard, Dufraisseix, Abbot, mark 6. *Courtesy of Bruce Guilmette*. $90-$125.

Dresser Tray, 14.75" x 12.5". Tressemanes & Vogt, mark 10. *Courtesy of Bruce Guilmette*. $150-$200.

Dresser Tray, 14.75" x 12.75". Tressemanes & Vogt, mark 10. *Courtesy of Bruce Guilmette*. $150-$200.

Tea Set: teapot, 4.5" high; creamer, 2.5" high; and sugar, 3.75" high. Guérin, mark 2 and overglaze, The Art China Decorating Company. $250-$275 for set.

Tea Set: teapot, 5.5" high; creamer, 3.5" high; sugar, 3.5" high; cups, 2.1" high; and saucers, 4.75" in diameter. Délinières, mark 2 and overglaze, Pickard; artist, signature illegible. *Courtesy of Dorla I. Battersby.* $300+ for set.

Tea Set: teapot, 8.5" high. Blakeman & Henderson, mark 2 and Coiffe, mark 3. *Courtesy of Bruce Guilmette.* $300-$350 for set.

Teapot, 6.25" high. Bower &
Dotter, mark 4; Redon, mark 5;
and MR impressed. $150-$175.

Teapot, 3.75" high. Paroutaud, mark 3. $80-$100.

Tea Set: teapot, 4.75"
high; creamer, 3.25"
high; and sugar, 3.75"
high. Haviland & Co.,
mark I and overglaze,
White's Art Company,
Chicago. *Courtesy of
Dorla I. Battersby.*
$250-$275 for set.

Teapot, 6" high. Pouyat, mark 7; artist, JRZ.
Courtesy of Bruce Guilmette. $150-$175.

Teapot, 3.5" high. Bernardaud, mark 3.
Courtesy of Bruce Guilmette. $100-$125.

Tea Set. Lanternier, marks 6 and 5. *Courtesy of Jane Abrams.* $300-$350 for set.

Teapot. Tressemanes & Vogt, mark 8 and overglaze, Plymouth [illegible] Flower. *Courtesy of Wayne and Robin Wechsler.* $100-$125.

Tea Set. Ahrenfeldt, mark 5 for teapot, creamer and sugar and Ahrenfeldt, mark 7 for cups and saucers. *Courtesy of Bruce Guilmette.* $450+ for set.

Tea and Luncheon Set. Tressemanes & Vogt, mark 10 for teapot, cups, and saucers; Pouyat, mark 7 for creamer and sugar; and Limoges, mark 1 for plates; artist, E. Miler. *Courtesy of Bruce Guilmette.* Luncheon set for six, $800-$1,000.

Chocolate Set: chocolate pot, 12" high. Tressemanes & Vogt, mark 10; artist, Levey. *Courtesy of Bruce Guilmette.* $1,000-$1,500 for set.

Coffee Pot, 8.5" high. T. Haviland, mark n, with Théodore and not Theo. $175-$225.

Chocolate Pot, 10" high. Tressemanes & Vogt, mark 11. *Courtesy of Bruce Guilmette.* $175-$250.

Chocolate Pot, 12" high. Paroutaud, mark 3; artist, E. Burcer 1915. *Courtesy of Bruce Guilmette.* $300-$450.

Chocolate Pot, 12" high. Guérin, mark 4. *Courtesy of Bruce Guilmette.* $175-$225.

Chocolate Pot, 7.75" high. Limoges, mark 10; artist, ADC. *Courtesy of Bruce Guilmette.* $225-$250.

Chocolate Set: chocolate pot, 9" high. Haviland & Co., mark H for chocolate pot and cups and saucers and Lanternier, mark 5 for creamer and sugar. *Courtesy of Bruce Guilmette.* Setting for twelve, $1,300-$1,500.

Chocolate Set: chocolate pot, 9" high. Haviland & Co., mark F for chocolate pot and Haviland & Co., Mark I for cups and saucers and plate. *Courtesy of Bruce Guilmette.* $800-$1,000 for set.

Chocolate Set. Limoges, mark 17 and overglaze, Raphael Weill & Co., San Francisco. *Courtesy of Wayne and Robin Wechsler.* $800-$1,000 for set.

Chocolate Set: chocolate pot, 11.75" high and cups, 3" high. Gérard, Dufraisseix, Abbot, marks 5 and 6. *Courtesy of Bruce Guilmette.* $1,200-$1,400.

Above: Chocolate Set: chocolate pot, 9.5" high. Bawo & Dotter, mark 4. Setting for eight, $800-$1,000.

Above right: Matching Cup and Saucer: cup, 3" high and saucer, 5.1" in diameter. Haviland & Co., mark I.

Right: Covered Bouillon Cup and Saucer: cup, 4" high and saucer, 5.75" in diameter. Haviland & Co., marks c and I. *Courtesy of Yasumasa Tanano.* $175-$225.

Above: Cup and Saucer. Tressemanes and Vogt, mark 9 and overglaze, The Artistic Hand Painting Company. $75-$100.

Left: Demitasse Cups and Saucers: cup, 2.25" high and saucer, 5" in diameter. T. Haviland, marks r and P with PÂTE IVOIRE. Set of two, $125-$150.

Below left: Demitasse Cup and Saucer: cup, 1.75" high and saucer, 4.75" in diameter. Guérin, mark 4; artist, Towler. $150-$175.

Below right: Demitasse Cup and Saucer: cup, 2.5" high and saucer, 5" in diameter. Gérard, Dufraisseix, Abbot, mark 6 and overglaze, S & G Gump Co. *Courtesy of Yasumasa Tanano.* $50-$75.

Artist mark for
Demitasse Cup
and Saucer.

Demitasse Cup and Saucer: cup, 1.9" high and saucer, 4.4" in diameter. Bawo &
Dotter, mark 4 and overglaze artist mark, *see accompanying mark.* $275-$325.

Cup and Saucer: cup, 2.5" high and saucer, 5" in diameter.
Haviland & Co., mark D and *see* other accompanying
mark. *Courtesy of Yasumasa Tanano.* $300+.

FABRIQUÉ PAR
HAVILAND&C?
d'après les dessins
DE
THÉODORE.R.DAVIS

Additional mark for
Cup and Saucer.

Cup and Saucer: cup, 2"
high and saucer, 4.25"
in diameter. Giraud,
mark 2. $20-$40.

Six Demitasse Cups and Saucers: cups, 2" high and saucers, 4.4" in diameter. Le Tallec, marks 1 and 2, before date marks began in 1941. $2,200+ for set.

Demitasse Cups and Saucers: cups, 2.25" high and saucers, 5" in diameter. Cup and saucer on left, T. Haviland, mark T and marked Garden Flowers and cup and saucer on right, T. Haviland, marks q and Q ; artist, S. Patry-Bie. *Courtesy of Yasumasa Tanano.* $45-$65 for set on left and $125-$150 for set on right.

Demitasse Cup, 2.5" high. Gutherz, mark 2. $75-$100.

Cup and Saucer: cup, 2" high and saucer, 5.5" in diameter. Gérard, Dufraisseix, Abbot, marks 7 and 6. *Courtesy of Yasumasa Tanano.* $45-$65.

Above: Demitasse Cup and Saucer: cup, 2" high and saucer, 4.4" in diameter. T. Haviland, marks O, with square line around mark and words Celadon China; M impressed, with three stars underneath mark; and o; artist, Suzanne Lalique. *Courtesy of Yasumasa Tanano.* $150+.

Left: View of Demitasse Cup and Saucer from top.

Above: Cup and Saucer; cup, 1.9" high and saucer, 5.5" in diameter. Gérard, Dufraisseix, Abbot, marks 5 and 6. $50-$75.

Right: Bouillon Cup and Saucer: cup, 2.1" high and saucer, 5.4" in diameter. Paroutaud, mark 3. $55-$65.

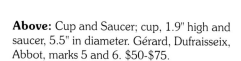

Cup and Saucer: cup, 2" high and saucer, 5.6" in diameter. Tressemanes & Vogt, mark 10; artist, G.S. Marlin. $50-$75.

Demitasse Cup and Saucer: cup, 2.25" high and saucer, 5" in diameter, Gérard, Dufraisseix & Morel, marks 2 and 1. *Courtesy of Yasumasa Tanano.* $75-$125.

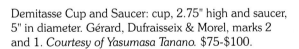

Demitasse Cup and Saucer: cup, 2.75" high and saucer, 5" in diameter. Gérard, Dufraisseix & Morel, marks 2 and 1. *Courtesy of Yasumasa Tanano.* $75-$100.

Cup and Saucer: cup, 2" high and saucer, 4.5" in diameter. Bawo & Dotter, mark 11. *Courtesy of Bruce Guilmette.* $75-$125.

Demitasse Cup and Saucer: cup, 2.4" high and saucer, 4.5" square, rare blanks. Pouyat, mark 3 for cup and Pouyat, mark 7 for saucer. $150-$225.

Above: Cup and Saucer: cup, 2" high and saucer, 5.75" in diameter. Ahrenfeldt, mark 6 on both cup and saucer and Ahrenfeldt, mark 5 on cup and mark 10 on saucer. $50-$60.

Right: Bouillon Cup and Saucer: cup, 2.1" high and saucer, 5.6" in diameter. Bernardaud, mark 4 and Délinières, mark 2. $60-$70.

Demitasse Cup and Saucer: cup, 2.75" high and saucer, 4.5" in diameter. Le Tallec, mark 3, 1960. Set of eight, $3,000+.

Bouillon Cup and Saucer: cup, 2.25" high and saucer, 6" in diameter. Bernardaud, mark 4 and Délinières, mark 2. $60-$70.

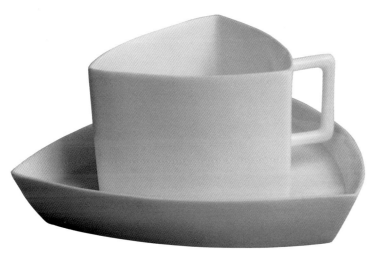

Mustache Cup: cup, 3.25" high and 3.5" in diameter and saucer, 6.25" in diameter. C.F. Haviland, mark 2 impressed. *Courtesy of Yasumasa Tanano*. $125-$175.

Demitasse Cup and Saucer: cup, 2" high and 3" on each side and saucer, 5" on each side. Pouyat, mark 3. *Courtesy of Yasumasa Tanano*. $75-$125.

Creamer and Sugar: sugar, 3.5" high and creamer, 2.5" high. Laviolette, mark 1 for creamer and Coiffe, mark 2 for sugar. $70-$85.

Sugar, 5.75" high. Tressemanes
& Vogt, mark 10. *Courtesy of
Bruce Guilmette.* $85-$125.

Sugar, 6" high. T. Haviland,
mark n, with Théodore
instead of Theo. $200-$225.

Above: Sugar, 5.5" high.
Coiffe, mark 3; artist, L.P.
Price. *Courtesy of Bruce
Guilmette.* $85-$125.

Right: Tea Caddy, 4.75"
high. Haviland & Co.
Courtesy of Tom Roth.
$150-$175.

Creamer, 3.5" high. Haviland &
Co., marks g and D. $30-$50.

Plate, 9.75" in diameter. T. Haviland, marks o, O with square line around mark and words Celadon China, and M impressed with three stars underneath; artist, Suzanne Lalique. *Courtesy of Yasumasa Tanano.* $200+.

Plate, 7.5" in diameter. T. Haviland, marks o, O with square line around mark and words Celadon China, and M impressed with three stars underneath; artist, Suzanne Lalique. *Courtesy of Yasumasa Tanano.* $150+.

Plates, 9" in diameter. Tressemanes & Vogt, mark 8; artist, L. B. Bradford. *Courtesy of Bruce Guilmette.* Set of eleven, $700-$1,000.

Plate, 9.5" in diameter. Paroutaud, mark 2 and Limoges, mark 1. $30-$35.

Plate, 9.5" in diameter. Haviland & Co.,
marks g and F. Set of eight, $400-$450.

Plate, 8.25" in diameter. Ahrenfeldt, mark 7.
Courtesy of Bruce Guilmette. $60-$70.

Plate, 8.5" in diameter. Pouyat, marks 8 and 7.
Courtesy of Bruce Guilmette. $65-$75.

Plate, 7.25" in diameter. Tressemanes & Vogt, mark 10; artist, V.
W. G. *Courtesy of Bruce Guilmette.* Set of nine, $350-$450.

Plate, 8.5" in diameter. Blakeman & Henderson,
mark 1 and Coiffe, mark 3. *Courtesy of Bruce
Guilmette*. Set of seven, $250-$325.

Plate, 9" in diameter. Haviland & Co., marks i and I.
Courtesy of Bruce Guilmette. Set of twelve, $700-$1,000.

Plate, 6.25" in diameter. Paroutaud, mark 3.
Courtesy of Bruce Guilmette. $25-$35.

Plate, 7.5" in diameter. C. F. Haviland, marks 1 and 3.
Courtesy of Yasumasa Tanano. $50-$75.

Above left: Plate, 8.5" in diameter. Ahrenfeldt, mark 11. *Courtesy of Bruce Guilmette.* Set of twelve, $500-$600.

Above right: Plate, 7.5" in diameter. Redon, marks 3 and 5. *Courtesy of Yasumasa Tanano.* $35-$50.

Left: Plate, 6.25" in diameter. Pouyat, mark 7; artist, E.J. Glass. *Courtesy of Bruce Guilmette.* Set of six, $150-$175.

Below: Bone Dish, 4.75" x 8.75". Gérard, Dufraisseix & Morel, marks 2 and 1. *Courtesy of Yasumasa Tanano.* $50-$75.

Oyster Plate, unusually large blank, 9.9" in diameter. Tressemanes & Vogt, marks 12, with JMᶜD&S as part of and over mark, and 8. *Courtesy of Dorla I. Battersby.* $425-$450.

Oyster Plate, 8.75" in diameter. Haviland & Co., mark F and overglaze, Haviland & Co. Pour Tiffany & Co., N.Y. *Courtesy of Yasumasa Tanano.* $250-$300.

Oyster Plate, 8.4" in diameter. Haviland & Co., mark F. $125-$150.

Orange Cup, 2.75" high, rare blank. Tressemanes & Vogt, mark 11. *Courtesy of Bruce Guilmette.* $125-$150.

Above: Orange Cup, 3.5" high, rare blank. Bawo & Dotter, mark 4. $150-$175.

Right: View inside of Orange Cup. Note three protruding hooks.

Platter, 18" x 12". Haviland & Co., mark H. *Courtesy of Bruce Guilmette*. $140-$160.

Platter, 14.75" x 10". Pouyat, mark 7; artist, Mieghorn. *Courtesy of Bruce Guilmette*. $125-$135.

Tray, 10.9" x 7.5". Gérard, Dufraisseix, mark 1; artist, S.F. Dwyer '93. $75-$90.

Platter, 18.5" x 11.5". Gérard, Dufraisseix, mark 1. *Courtesy of Bruce Guilmette.* $140-$160.

Tray, 13.75" long. Tressemanes & Vogt, mark 8. *Courtesy of Bruce Guilmette.* $125-$135.

Bowl, 15.75" long. Tressemanes & Vogt, mark 10. *Courtesy of Bruce Guilmette.* $175-$200.

Above: Celery Tray, 13" x 7.5". Pouyat, marks 5 and 7; artist, Duval. *Courtesy of Jacqueline Lowensteiner.* $150-$175.

Right: Celery or Relish Tray, 9.25" long. Limoges, mark 6. *Courtesy of Bruce Guilmette.* $90-$100.

Below: Tray, 5.75" x 5.5". Délinières, marks 3 and 2. $60-$85.

Dinnerware Set: platter, 11.5" x 8"; vegetable dish, 9" x 5.25"; and dessert bowls, 5" in diameter. Haviland & Co., mark I. *Courtesy of Bruce Guilmette.* $275-$300 for set.

Vegetable Dish, 11.75" x 7.5". Gérard, Dufraisseix, Abbot, marks 5 and 6. $125-$150.

Above: Serving Bowl, 7" high x 12" handle to handle. Raynaud, mark 10. $75-$125.

Right: Serving Dish: bowl and plate, 8.25" in diameter. Gérard, Dufraisseix, Abbot, marks 1 for bowl and 6 for plate. $165-$180.

Above: Salad Bowl, 11.75" x 9.25". Haviland & Co., mark F and overglaze, 1869, 1889. $125-$175.

Right: Pudding Set: bowl, 9" in diameter and plate, 11.75" in diameter. Tressemanes & Vogt, mark 10 and Lanternier, mark 5 impressed on both bowl and plate; Lanternier, mark 5 in green on plate and A.L. Déposé in green on bowl. $225-$250.

Left: Serving Bowl, 7.75" square. R. Haviland, mark 4. $95-$125.

Below: Bowl, 8.75" in diameter. Limoges, mark 1 and overglaze, Claremore Art Studio, HP. $50-$60.

Above: Bowl. Pouyat, mark 7. *Courtesy of Jane Abrams.* $80-$95.

Left: Serving Bowl, 11.5" x 7.5". Haviland & Co., mark g and one of the H&C° marks. *Courtesy of Tom Roth.* $225-$275.

Below: Cheese Dish: dome, 5.5" square and plate, 8" square. Gérard, Dufraisseix, & Morel, marks 2 and 1. *Courtesy of Yasumasa Tanano.* $275-$350.

Mustard Pot, 3.4" high. Tressemanes
& Vogt, mark 10. $75-$100.

Mustard Pot, 1.9" high.
Pouyat, mark 7. $75-$100.

Sectional Dish, 11.5" in diameter. Union Céramique, marks 2
and 1. *Courtesy of Yasumasa Tanano.* $50-$75.

Above: Sectional Dish, 10.5" in
diameter. Haviland & Co., mark H and
rare decorating mark with Haviland in
gold script. *Courtesy of Yasumasa
Tanano.* $250-$325.

Above: Salt and Pepper Shakers, 4.4" high. T. Haviland, mark R. *Courtesy of Yasumasa Tanano.* $75-$100 for set.

Right: Toothpick Holder, 3.5" long. Pouyat, mark 7. $70-$90.

Below left: Trivet, 6.75" in diameter. Gérard, Dufraisseix, Abbot, marks 5 and 6. *Courtesy of Yasumasa Tanano.* $40-$75.

Below right: Hors d'Oeuvre Plate, 8" in diameter. Lazarus Straus & Sons, mark 1 and Mavaleix & Granger, mark 1. *Courtesy of Yasumasa Tanano.* $75-$100.

Above: Bonbon Dish, 8.75" x 6".
Pouyat, mark 7 and overglaze, Hand
Painted Stouffer. $65-$80.

Right: Bonbon Dish, 10" x 8.5".
Pouyat, mark 7; artist, Hattie 1905.
$55-$70.

Above: Bonbon Dish, 10.6" x 7".
Guérin, mark 4. $55-$70.

Right: Bonbon Dish or Sauce Boat,
5.5" in diameter. Pouyat, mark 7.
Courtesy of Bruce Guilmette. $65-$80.

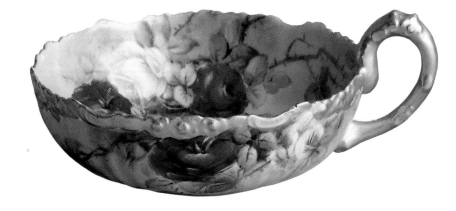

Above left: Relish Dish, 8" x 9.25". Haviland & Co., marks a and F. *Courtesy of Yasumasa Tanano*. $100-$150.

Above right: Hors d'Oeuvre Plate, 8.5" x 7.5". Haviland & Co., mark H. *Courtesy of Bruce Guilmette*. $50-$60.

Left: Bowl, 2.5" high and 6.6" in diameter. Tressemanes & Vogt, mark 10. $55-$70.

Ice Cream Dish, 6" x 7.5". Gérard, Dufraisseix, marks 2 and 1. *Courtesy of Yasumasa Tanano*. $100-$125.

Ice Cream Dish, 6" x 8". Gérard, Dufraisseix, & Morel, marks 2 and 1. *Courtesy of Yasumasa Tanano.* $125-$175.

Ice Cream Dish, 6" x 8". Gérard, Dufraisseix, & Morel, mark 1. *Courtesy of Yasumasa Tanano.* $125-$175.

Ice Cream Dish, 6" x 8", Gérard, Dufraisseix, mark 1. *Courtesy of Yasumasa Tanano.* $125-$175.

Ice Cream Dish, 6" x 8". Gérard, Dufraisseix, & Morel, marks 2 and 1. *Courtesy of Yasumasa Tanano.* $125-$175.

Cake Plate, 11.75" in diameter. Borgfeldt, mark 1 and Mavaleix, mark 1; artist, Ted Alfred Broussilon. $200-$250.

Cake Plate, 12" in diameter. Paroutaud, mark 3; artist, G. Lykes. *Courtesy of Bruce Guilmette*. $175-$250.

Cake Plate, 9.25" in diameter. Gérard, Dufraisseix, Abbot, mark 6. *Courtesy of Bruce Guilmette*. $125-$150.

Cake Plate, 10.75" in diameter. Tressemanes & Vogt, mark 10. *Courtesy of Bruce Guilmette*. $175-$225.

Cake Plate, 13" in diameter. T. Haviland, marks q and M impressed. *Courtesy of Bruce Guilmette.* $225-$250.

Cake Plate, 10" in diameter. Bawo & Dotter, mark 1. $125-$150.

Cake Plate, 10.6" in diameter Délinières, mark 2. $50-$60.

Cake Plate, 11" in diameter. Pouyat, mark 7. *Courtesy of Bruce Guilmette.* $200-$250.

Biscuit Jar, 7.25" high. Gérard, Dufraisseix, & Morel, mark 1. *Courtesy of Yasumasa Tanano.* $150-$200.

Biscuit Jar, 7.25" high. Tressemanes & Vogt, mark 3. $75-$100.

Cider Pitcher and Six Cups: pitcher, 6.5" high and cups, 3/5" high. Pouyat, mark 7; artist, E. Miler. *Courtesy of Bruce Guilmette.* $450-$600.

Cider Pitcher and Eight Cups: pitcher, 6.5" high and cups, 2.5" high. Guérin, mark 4; artist, I.L. Brunner 1912. *Courtesy of Bruce Guilmette.* $500-$700.

Cider Pitcher and Six Cups: pitcher, 6.5" high and cups, 4.25" high. Bernardaud, mark 1 and overglaze, 9/29/13. *Courtesy of Bruce Guilmette*. $800-$1,000.

Cider Pitcher and Four Cups: pitcher, 6.5" high and cups, 4" high. Pouyat, mark 5 on pitcher and no marks on cups. *Courtesy of Bruce Guilmette*. $250-$300.

Cider Pitcher, 6" high. Guérin, mark 4. $65-$75.

Pitcher, 4.75" high. Pouyat, mark 5.
Courtesy of Bruce Guilmette. $100-$150.

Pitcher, 6.5" high, with pewter top. C. F.
Haviland, mark 2 impressed. *Courtesy of
Yasumasa Tanano*. $75-$100.

Water Pitcher, 11" high. Alluaud, mark 1
impressed, very rare mark. $450+.

Ewer, 9" high, uncommon pottery piece. Mark
similar to Haviland & Co, mark C impressed.
$1,000-$1,500.

Pitcher, 12" high, Tressemanes
& Vogt, mark 8. *Courtesy of
Bruce Guilmette*. $450-$500.

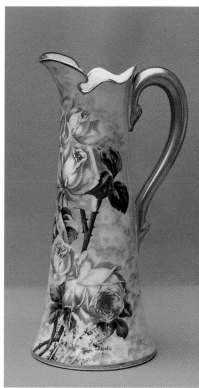

Tankard, 16.75" high, Bower & Dotter, marks 10 and 11. *Courtesy of Bruce Guilmette*. $750-$1,000.

Pitcher, 8" high. Tressemanes & Vogt, mark 8. *Courtesy of Bruce Guilmette*. $300-$450.

Pitcher. Blakeman & Henderson, mark 1. *Courtesy of Bruce Guilmette*. $500-$700.

Above: Tankard and Mug: tankard, 10.25" high and mug, 5.5" high. Pouyat, mark 7. *Courtesy of Yasumasa Tanano*. $175-$225 for tankard; $50-$75 for mug.

Right: Tankard and Five Mugs: tankard, 14.75" high and mugs, 5.5" high. Pouyat, mark 7 and overglaze, Hand Painted Stouffer; artist signature illegible. $1,250-$1,700.

Tankard and Six Mugs: tankard, 14.5" high and mugs,
5.5" high. Pouyat, mark 7. $1,000-$1,250.

Mug, 5.75" high.
Porcelaine Limousine,
mark 1. $60-$80.

Mug, 5.1" high. Pouyat, mark 7 and
overglaze, White's Art Company,
Chicago, Hand Painted. *Courtesy of
Dorla I. Battersby.* $60-$80.

Two Goblets, 4.9" high. Giraud, mark 5
and Limoges, mark 3. $30-$40.

Above: Punch Bowl with Stand, 13" in diameter and 8.5" high. Tressemanes & Vogt, mark 11. *Courtesy of Bruce Guilmette.* $2,000-$3,000.

Right: Bowl and Plate: bowl, 14" in diameter and 7" high, plate 15.5" in diameter. Tressemanes & Vogt, mark 10. *Courtesy of Bruce Guilmette.* $2,000-$3,000.

Above: Punch Bowl. Tressemanes & Vogt, mark 10. *Courtesy of Bruce Guilmette.* $1,500-$2,500.

Right: Inside of Punch Bowl.

Left: Punch Bowl and Stand, 13.75" in diameter and 9" high. Tressemanes & Vogt, mark 6 for bowl and Tressemanes & Vogt, mark 8 for stand. *Courtesy of Bruce Guilmette*. $1,500-$1,700.

Below: Punch Bowl, 13" in diameter and 6" high. Tressemanes & Vogt, mark 10. *Courtesy of Bruce Guilmette*. $1,500-$2,500.

Punch Bowl and Eight Cups: bowl, 15" in diameter and 9" high and cups, 3.25" high. Tressemanes & Vogt, mark 10 for bowl and no mark for cups. *Courtesy of Bruce Guilmette*. $2,000-$3,000.

Punch Bowl and Stand, 14" in diameter and 9.5" high. Tressemanes & Vogt, marks 12 and 11. *Courtesy of Bruce Guilmette*. $2,700-$3,500.

Punch Bowl with Eight Cups: bowl, 11" in diameter and 4.75" high and cups, 3.5" high. Pouyat, mark 5. *Courtesy of Bruce Guilmette*. $1,000-$1,500.

Punch Bowl, 16" in diameter and 6.75" high, unusually large blank. Tressemanes & Vogt, mark 10. $1,000-$1,200.

Punch Bowl with Tray: bowl, 16" in diameter and 7" high, unusually large blank, Guérin, mark 2. *Courtesy of Bruce Guilmette*. $1,800-$2,200.

Punch Cup, 4.9" high. Florale, mark 1. $30-$40.

Punch Cup, 5.25" high. Délinières, mark 2. $25-$30.

Punch Cup, 5.1" high. Tressemanes & Vogt, marks 12 and 10. $30-$40.

Platter, 15.75" x
11.25", rare subject.
Flambeau, mark 5
and Coiffe, mark 3.
$250-$300.

Fish Platter and Five Plates: platter, 16.5"
x 12.75" and plates, 8.5" in diameter.
Blakeman & Henderson, mark 2 and
Limoges, mark 3; artist, Luc. $650-$750.

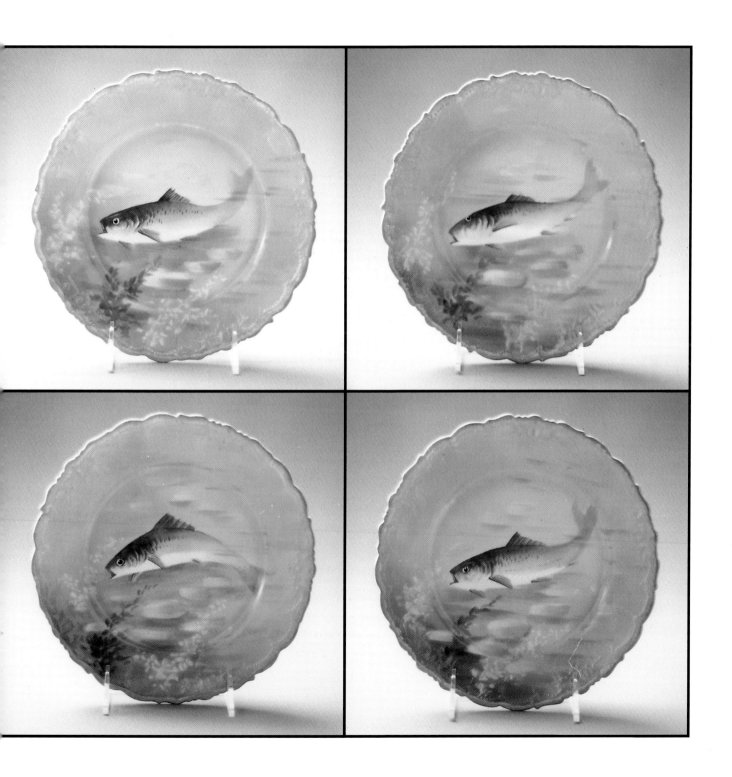

Fish Plates and Gravy
Boat: plates, 9.25" in
diameter and gravy boat
and saucer, 4.5" high x
8.75" x 6.1". Leonard,
mark 1 and V.F., mark 1.
Set of four plates and
gravy boat. $375-$425.

Fish Plate, 9" in diameter. T. Haviland, mark o; artist, J. Martin.
Courtesy of Yasumasa Tanano. $125-$150.

Seafood Dish, 10.5" x 5.75". Tressemanes &
Vogt, mark 11; artist, ACS. $125-$150.

Game Platter, 19" x 13". Borgfeldt, mark 1 and Coiffe, mark 2; artist,
Duval. *Courtesy of Jacqueline Lowensteiner.* $175-$200.

Game Set: platter, 18" x 11"; plates, 9" in diameter; and relish/sauce
dishes, 6" long. Borgfeldt, mark 1. *Courtesy of Tom Roth*. Set of
platter, twelve plates and two jelly dishes, $2,500-$3,000.

Above: Game Platter and Two Plates: platter, 18" and 10.5" and plates, 9.25" in diameter. Lazarus Straus & Sons, mark 1 and Limoges, mark 8. $300-$350.

Opposite: Six Game Plates, 8.5" in diameter. Blakeman & Henderson, mark 2; artist, Dubois. $200-$250.

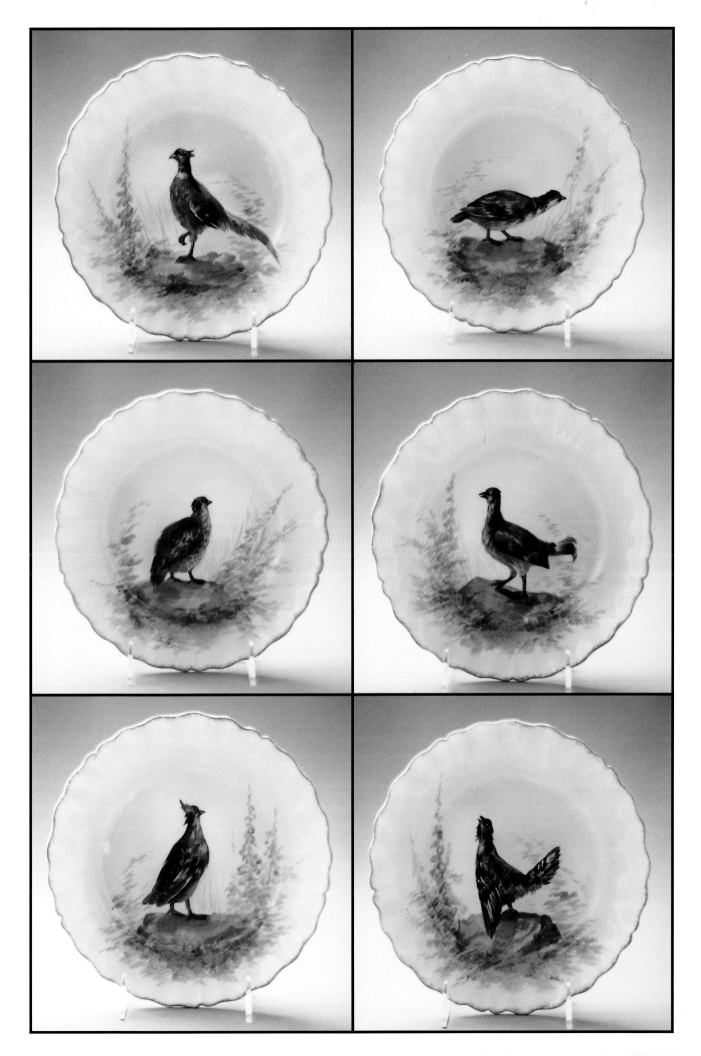

Game Set: platter, 16.5" x 10.5" and plates, 9" in diameter. Haviland &
Co., mark g and one of the H&Co. marks. *Courtesy of Tom Roth.* Set
of platter and twelve plates, $3,000-$4,000.

Part II. Limoges Boxes

The contemporary Limoges boxes were first exported to the United States in the early 1960s by Charles Martine, who started his own export firm in 1955. Mr. Martine, who died in September 1996, is credited with first introducing and popularizing Limoges boxes in the U.S., which is the largest market for Limoges boxes in the world. In was not until about 1980, however, that Limoges boxes were widely embraced by U.S. collectors; since that time, however, the number and variety of boxes have increased dramatically.

Since most of the old hand-enameled boxes and the old porcelain boxes are currently in private collections and in museums, and very few appear in auctions or on the secondary market, we have focused our attention on those boxes that are widely available to collectors. Today, contemporary Limoges boxes are available from numerous sources—upscale department stores, gift shops and catalogues, web site dealer pages and auctions, some discount warehouses, and the Home Shopping Network and QVC on television.

With many of the Limoges boxes that are currently available, it is impossible to identify the manufacturing company that produced them or the studio or artist that decorated them. Some companies, like Rochard and Dubarry, are simply importers and not manufacturers or decorators, even though the name, Rochard and Dubarry, is painted on the boxes. Companies like Rochard and Dubarry buy boxes from several Limoges companies for import. Other companies, like Chamart (Charles Martine), buy all their blanks from different porcelain manufacturers, but do their own decorating and importing. Artoria, on the other hand, manufactures, decorates and exports their own boxes, while they sell their blanks to many other decorating and exporting companies. While there are about a dozen manufacturers of Limoges box blanks, there are two to three times as many decorating companies, most of which are very small and many are not identified. A decorating studio of 15 people is considered very large; most have many fewer people. With these smaller companies, the boxes are simply painted, *Limoges France* (some have an actual underglaze green ware mark) with the accompanying words, *peint main*, *peint à la mein* or *hand-painted*.

Because our primary focus is on well painted and decorated Limoges porcelain, we have not attempted to provide photographs that are representative of the wide variety of available boxes, which number in the thousands. Rather, we have concentrated on, what for a better term, we might call "high end" boxes. These include both subject-shaped boxes and traditional-shaped boxes. With our emphasis on decorative craftsmanship, we have included several pieces from the decorating studio, Le Tallec, now owned by Tiffany & Co.; S&D Limoges; Chamart; Rochard; and Artoria. In addition to Le Tallec, Ancienne Manufacture Royale makes exquisite reproductions of 18th and 19th century boxes. In addition, certain retail stores, like Lucy Zahran in Beverly Hills and Costa Mesa and Gump's in San Francisco, are now participating in the design and development of their own exclusive and limited edition boxes that must meet unusually high decorating standards. These stores contract with companies, like S&D Limoges, Chamart or Rochard, who in turn work with companies in Limoges to produce boxes that are unique in terms of decoration and often in shape as well.

History of Limoges Boxes

Beginning in the Middle Ages, through the Renaissance, and up until the middle of the 17th century, Limoges was famous for its goldsmith work and enamels. True Limoges enamels, so called painted enamels, were invented in the second half of the 15th century. Following this tradition of painted enamels, present day porcelain Limoges boxes were preceded by painted enamel tobacco boxes called *tabatières,* or snuff boxes, which were popular with upper class French society in the latter half of the 18th century. During the French Revolution, 1789–1799, the art of enameling was abandoned and the artists who painted these boxes fled to other countries. While the first known piece of porcelain made in Limoges, France, dates from 1771, the first porcelain Limoges boxes did not appear until some-time later during the first part of the 19th century. Other companies outside of Limoges did, however, produce porcelain boxes somewhat earlier, beginning in the 18th century. These companies included Sèvres and St. Cloud near Paris and Meissen in Germany. The old enamel boxes and early porcelain boxes were much more limited in the variety of shapes than the boxes of today. These older boxes were usually shaped as rectangles, ovals, hearts or eggs and were decorated with flowers, fruit, fish and cherubs and often finished with gold accents. Although some of today's boxes are reproductions of these earlier boxes, there are now an almost infinite number of shapes and designs that appeal to a broad spectrum of collectors, many with special interests.

Quality of Decoration

The key question is how does the collector place a value on the thousands of Limoges boxes that are currently available? There are several criteria that must be evaluated. For starters, certain well known companies, like Rochard, Artoria, S&D Limoges and Chamart, have a history of providing boxes that are usually of high quality. The decorating studio, Le Tallec, for example, produces a relatively small number of boxes, but their decorating is consistently exquisite. In all of these cases, the name of the company gives some indication of quality and value and provides assurance that the boxes were decorated in France. Decorating method can also help to determine the value of a particular box. As with other kinds of Limoges porcelain, there are three basic styles of decorating: (1) boxes that are entirely hand-painted, (2) boxes that are decorated with transfers or decals only and (3) boxes that exhibit both methods, which is called "mixed," because they incorporate both transfers and hand-painting. The painting in the mixed method is usually applied to add a certain emphasis or highlight to the transfer. Many boxes, although labeled *hand-painted*, are, upon closer inspection, largely spray painted or are decorated with both transfers and hand-painted highlights. This is a new twist to the definition of hand-painted and is misleading. Generally, boxes that are entirely painted by hand are more likely to increase in value. All boxes marked *Le Tallec, Artoria* and *Chamart* are totally hand-painted, as well as those boxes imported by S&D Limoges. As with any painting, the collector must learn to evaluate the quality of the painting itself—the amount of detail, style, colors, proportions and how well the painting fits with the shape of the box.

The painting inside the box is to a lesser extent also important in determining value. While some boxes have very detailed and attractive paintings inside and are sought after for this reason, as well, others have no painting inside at all. Questions to ask are, is it well painted and does the painting relate to the subject painted on the outside of the box? Or is the painting inside just a generic painting of, say, a wisp of leaf with no relationship to the subject of the box? A simple example of a box where there is a relationship between the subject of the box and the inside decoration would be a parrot box with peanuts painted inside. Here the two are related because parrots eat peanuts. Similarly, an ark box has a dove with an olive branch painted inside, because the dove represents the appearance of land. Yet another variation are those boxes that have a removable piece inside, in addition to or in place of an inside decoration. For example, there is a box of Notre Dame Cathedral that contains a removable hand-painted figure of the Hunchback. This box, of course, is commemorating Victor Hugo's story *The Hunchback of Notre Dame.*

Another important characteristic in evaluating the quality of a box is the brass hardware, which may come in several finishes, including polished, antiqued and burnished black. Hardware that must be fitted to porcelain boxes that have unusual shaped rims —i.e., they are not round, oval, square or rectangle—can add significantly to the cost of production. Questions to ask about the hardware are, does the trim fit snugly to the porcelain and does the trim on the bottom and top of the box line up evenly when the box is closed? Also, does the hammered clasp relate to the subject of the box itself or is the clasp a generic one, such as a nondescript flower or other simple design? For example, a seal box may have a fish for a clasp, since fish are a food staple for seals; or a Halloween witch box may have a half moon clasp, because witches are creatures of the night. Even so, while some boxes of mediocre decoration have cleverly designed clasps, other boxes with exquisite decoration have only generic-shaped clasps, so the clasps by themselves are by no means a major means of determining value. Boxes that are reproductions of earlier pieces often have simple clasps. The design of the clasp is only one indication of the amount of overall detail put into the decoration of the box.

Characteristics

Certain blanks and decorating schemes were more widely produced than others. In such cases, scarcity of a particular box can add value. For example, the box of a rabbit coming out of an egg is available everywhere in a wide variety of colors and painting schemes, while a box of a large dinosaur is relatively scarce. Boxes marked *Artoria*, for example, are blanks unique only to Artoria, while boxes bearing their green ware mark *Limoges* in a half moon with *France* underneath, are sold to numerous decorating studios. On the other hand, about half the blanks used by Chamart are exclusive to Chamart. Other collectors only consider boxes that are part of limited editions, which is usually written on the bottom of the box. "Limited edition," however, many times indicates that a certain painting scheme is limited and not the blank it is painted on. More frequently, however, the box is numbered with no indication of the total number of boxes in the edition.

Whether a box is signed or not also helps to determine its values. Some collectors only want boxes that are artist signed, even though the "signature" is more often than not the initials of an unidentified artist who may or may not be a good painter. A few boxes, on the other hand, will include the actual name of the artist. In most instances, the initials of the artist are painted on the bottom of the box; sometimes the initials or signature of the artist are on the painting itself.

Certain boxes demand higher prices because royalties must be paid to reproduce materials that are copyrighted. The most notable examples are boxes of Walt Disney™ characters, such as Mickey Mouse™ and Donald Duck™. Added to the normal costs of these boxes are the additional costs of paying royalties to the Walt Disney Company for reproducing their characters. Although these boxes might be more expensive, they are generally very well detailed and very well painted and are true representations of the characters, not crude imitations. More and more examples of Limoges boxes of copyrighted materials are appearing, such as Peanuts™, Barbie™ and Betty Boop™. Most of the boxes of copyrighted materials are being produced by Artoria.

The most important factor in determining the value of a particular box, however, is the overall quality of the detail and decoration. There are also other intangible factors that determine value, and these mostly have to do with individual taste and popularity of a particular theme at any given time. There is no accounting for taste, as they say; nevertheless, certain popular themes can be detected. For example, boxes that contain removable pieces are currently popular and command higher prices. Certain subjects, like dogs and cats, and certain shapes, like eggs and hearts, are also popular and more in demand.

One word of caution, however. Thousands of boxes rejected as seconds by companies in Limoges are appearing and being dumped on the market at significantly lower prices. Also, thousands of Limoges box blanks are being exported to the U.S. and elsewhere. Some companies represent that their boxes are painted by "famous" painters. These painters, in fact, are not French Limoges painters but amateur painters in the U.S. Some of these same companies also offer classes in learning how to become a porcelain painter. For the most part, boxes that have been painted in Limoges, or by other professional decorators, will hold their value much better than boxes painted by amateurs in the U.S., although this may change over time as boxes begin falling into the category of antiques. Since it is not always easy to tell the decorating origin of the box, serious collectors would be wise to purchase boxes from the better known companies. (Boxes bearing the words, *Limoges France*, under the glaze only attest that the porcelain, not the decoration, originates in Limoges. *Peint main* or *peint à la mein*, although indicating the box is hand-painted, does not, even through written in French, guarantee that it was painted in Limoges, or elsewhere in France, or that it is entirely hand-painted, as noted earlier.)

Because the quality of decoration of Limoges boxes is associated with five major companies, we have grouped the photographs in this section by company. We have also included a section named "Other," which includes boxes from additional companies and boxes that are not marked with the name of any company. The only company of the five that does not mark its boxes with the company name is S&D Limoges. Hopefully, the company will at some point change this policy, since they distribute some of the finest Limoges boxes in the U.S.

Many of the Limoges boxes pictured in this chapter are still available from retail stores, and the values on the secondary market in many instances still approximate the retail prices. Because these prices vary, however, depending upon where the boxes are purchased, the collector can expect to pay as much as 30% less than the values listed for some of the boxes, although a variance of 15% to 20% would be more likely. This is not the case, however, with the older Le Tallec boxes, where the values are stated in ranges.

Artoria Limoges

All boxes are marked *Artoria*.

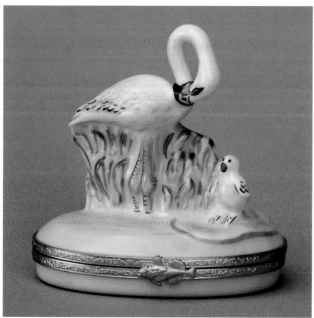

Above left: Parrot, 3" high. $160.

Above: Toucan, 2.75" high. $160.

Left: Flamingos, 3" high. $145.

Far left:
Cockatoo, 3"
high. $130.

Left: Wood-
pecker, 3" high.
$145.

Far Left:
Humpty
Dumpty, 2.75"
high. $195.

Left:
Cinderella's™
Dress, 3" high.
$165.

Far left:
Cinderella's
Slipper, 2.25"
high. $185.

Left: Mrs.
Potts™, 3" high.
$185.

Mickey™ and Minnie™ on Sleigh, 3" high. *Courtesy of Artoria Limoges*. $345.

Minnie on Piano, 3.6" high. *Courtesy of Artoria Limoges*. $235.

Mickey in Car, 2.5" high. *Courtesy of Artoria Limoges*. $340.

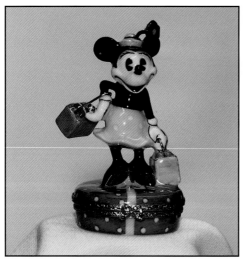

Minnie Shopping. *Courtesy of Lucy Zahran & Company*. $335.

Pluto™ with Golf Caddie, 2.5" high. *Courtesy of Lucy Zahran & Company*. $320.

Daisy™ and Donald™ on Couch. *Courtesy of Lucy Zahran & Company*. $490.

Pluto in Dog House. *Courtesy of Lucy Zahran & Company*. $275.

Flying Bat, 2" high. $145.

Haunted House, 2.5" high. $160.

Roast Turkey, 1.5" high. *Courtesy of Artoria Limoges.* $140.

Love Birds, 2.25" high. *Courtesy of Artoria Limoges.* $145.

Stagecoach, 2.25" high. $180.

Lady Tourist, 3.2" high. *Courtesy of Lucy Zahran & Company.* $190.

Tropical Drink, 4" high. *Courtesy of Lucy Zahran & Company.* $220.

Red Barn. *Courtesy of Lucy Zahran & Company,* $245.

Boxes in this photograph were produced from 1969 to 1990. The identity and value of the boxes are from left to right, beginning with the back row. Row 1: Round Rooster Box, 2" high x 5" in diameter, $390; Chestnut Pot, 2" high, $175; Mushrooms, 2" high, $215; Orange/Blue Carlos, 2" high x 5.5" x 4", $375. Row 2: Louis XV Chantilly, 2" high x 5.5" x 3", $285; Snuff Box Hen and Rooster, 2" high x 4.5" x 3", $245; Clam Shell, 1" high x 4.5" x 3", $325. Row 3: Pea Pod, 4.5" long, $175; Sabot, 3.5" long, $250; Heart Peony, 3" high, $295. Row 4: Gold Lemon with Insects, 2" high, $225; Floral Sèvres Box, 1" high, $225; Oval Pansy Relief, 2" high, $235; Mr. & Mrs. Denis, 3" long, $245; Shell Box Dancers, 2" high, $195. Row 5: Strawberries, 1" high, $120; Gold Polychrome Gold Fish, 2" high, $200; "I Love You" Trunk, 1.5" high, $140; Black Sèvres Box, 3" long, $275. *Photographs are provided courtesy of Chamart/Charles Martine Imports, and all boxes are marked Chamart.*

Boxes in this photograph were produced from 1990 to 1998. The identity and value of the boxes are from left to right, beginning with the back row. Row 1: Pig with Apron, 3.5" high, $240; Cheetah, 3.5" high, $185; Sitting Tiger, 1" high, $210; Sailboat, 4.5" high, $180. Row 2: Commodore Duck, 4" high, $235; Cheese Dome, 2" high, $185; Elephant, 2.5" high, $185; Rabbit with Fall Leaves, 4" high, $170. Row 3: Tulips, 2.5" high, $170; Watering Can, 2.5" high, $180; Bowl with Pitcher, 2.5" high, $185; Gentleman Frog, 4" high, $265. Row 4: Valise Dog, 2.5" high, $195; Perfume Egg, 2" high, $190; Fine Cigars, 2.5" wide, $185. *Photographs are provided courtesy of Chamart/Charles Martine Imports, and all boxes are marked* Chamart.

Le Tallec

All boxes are marked with *Le Tallec*, mark 3.

Chinoiserie Box, 4.4"
wide x 1.75" deep.
*Courtesy of Lucy
Zahran & Company.*
$650.

Side of Chinoiserie
Box.

Heart Box, 3.25" at
widest points. 1987.
*Courtesy of Lucy
Zahran & Company.*
$550.

Above left: Oval Box, 2" high x 3.5" wide. Marked Tiffany & Co. Private Stock, 1986. $600-$700.

Above: Napoleonic Palms Round Box, 2.1" high and 2.1" in diameter. *Courtesy of Lucy Zahran & Company.* $450.

Left: Grape and Floral Round Box, 2.1" high and 2.1" in diameter. Design painted for Camille Le Tallec's daughter. 1991. Limited edition of 50. $450.

Gold Leaf Box, 5.1" wide x 3.4" deep.
Limoges Castel, mark 2. 1964. $600-$750.

Blue Oval Box, 5" high. Marked
Bonwit Teller. 1964. $600-$750.

Chinoiserie Box, 5.1" wide x 3.4" deep.
Limoges Castel, mark 2. 1955. $700-$900.

Heart Box, 3.5" at widest points.
1966. $600-$800.

Floral and Yellow Accented Box, 5.1" wide x 3.4" deep.
Marked Tiffany & Co. Private Stock. Limoges Castel, mark 2.
1967. *Courtesy of Jacqueline Lowensteiner*. $600-$750.

Rochard

All boxes are marked *Rochard.*

Piano, 2" high. $320.

Steeplechase, 2.4" high. *Courtesy of Rochard.* $390.

Man on Horseback, 1.75" square. $150.

Hunting Scene, 2.25" square. $150.

Santa with Children, 2.75" high. *Courtesy of Rochard.* $350.

Mermaid, 3" high. *Courtesy of Rochard*. $180.

Dog and Cat in Armchairs, 2.75" high. *Courtesy of Rochard*. $180 each.

Dinosaur, 4" high. $175.

Terrier in Gift Box, 2.75". $190.

Hippopotamus, 1.75" high. $180.

Seal, 2.5" wide. $160.

Dolphin, 3.4" high. $160.

Toucan and Parrot Egg, 3.75" high. *Courtesy of Rochard.* $490.

Noah's Ark, 2.25" high. *Courtesy of Rochard.* $350.

Parrot Head, 2.4" high. *Courtesy of Rochard.* $160.

Bird and Bath, 2.5" high.
Courtesy of Rochard. $250.

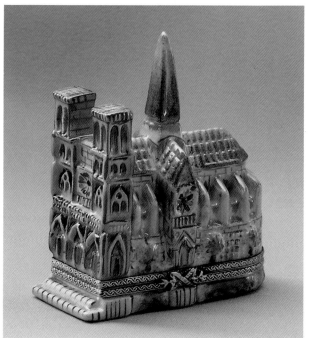

Notre Dame, 3.5" high.
Courtesy of Rochard. $250.

Above: Chateau, 2" high.
Courtesy of Rochard. $490.

Right: Chateau opened.

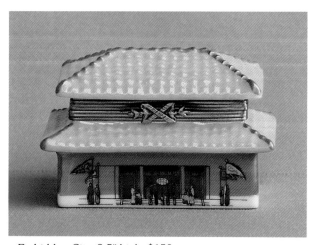

Forbidden City, 2.5" high. $150.

Box Roses, 3" wide. $120.

Harvest Egg, 6"
high. *Courtesy
of Rochard.*
$600.

Globe with Lions, 3.25" high. $260.

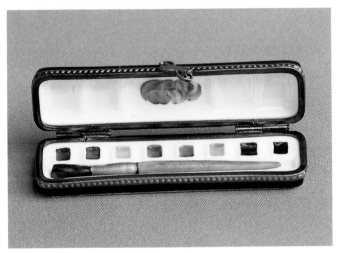

Paint Set, 3.5" wide. $170.

Clusters of Fruit, 2.9" wide.
Courtesy of Rochard. $200.

Christmas Tureen, 2.25" high.
Courtesy of Rochard. $160.

Versailles Egg, 2.1" high. *Courtesy of Rochard.* $180.

S & D Limoges

All photographs are provided courtesy of S&D Limoges.

Left: Imperial Court Monkey, 2.75" high. Limited edition of 500. $370.

Below: Opera Glasses, 2.4" x 0.75". $220.

Winged Cherub,
2.25" high.
Limited edition
of 300. $230.

Grand Imperial Egg, 3.75" high.
Limited edition of 250. $690.

Pastime Panorama, 6.5" high.
Limited edition of 250. $445.

Fiddling Frog, 4" high,
$240.

Frog Goes A Courting,
1.5" high. $165.

Hunting Stein, 4" high. $240.

Gainsborough Hunter, 2.75" high. $190.

Versailles Oval Box, 2.5" x 1.5". $280.

Directoire Box, 2.25" high. $165

Versailles Rectangular Box, 3" x 1.1".
Limited edition of 250. $280.

Cinderella's Washing Pail,
2.5" high. $160.

Seated Fox, 3.5" high.
$310.

Louis XV Table, 2" high. $260.

Victorian Triple Back Settee, 2.5" wide. $230.

Antiquarian Stack of Books, 2.75" high. $260.

Sèvres Angel, 2.75" high. $180.

Louis XVI Cabriole Chair. $210.

Louis XVI Cabriole Leg Settee, 2" wide. $250.

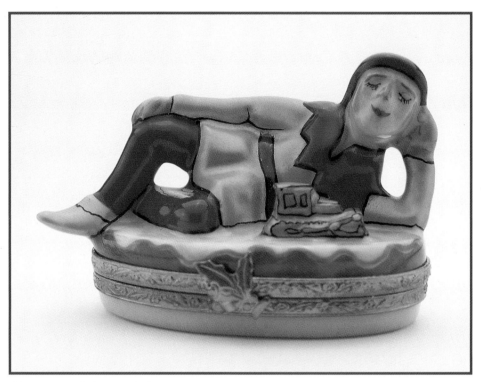

Christmas Elf, 2.4" wide. $185.

Yuletide Egg, 3.75" high. $375.

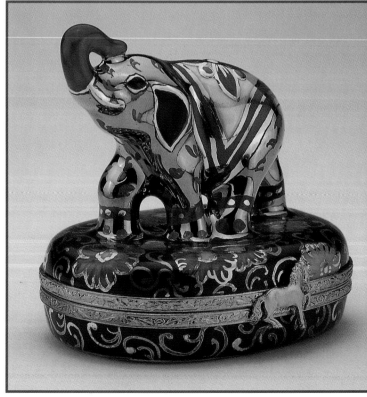

Asian Elephant, 2.5" high. Limited edition of 500. $235.

Above: Cinderella's Carriage, 2.25" high. $200.

Left: Old World Santa, 4.75" high. $210.

Other Boxes

All boxes in this section are marked *Limoges, France*, many with the initials of the decorator. Where noted, some boxes are also marked with the name of a company.

Far left: Swan, 2" high. Fabergé, mark $180.

Left: The Chick in the Imperial Hen Egg by Fabergé, 1.5" high. Fabergé, mark 1. $1...

Far left: The King's Cat (le chat du roi), 1.5" high. Ancienne Manufacture Royal, mark 15. $175.

Left: Back of the King's Cat box.

Foo Dog, 4" high. $270.

Mr. and Mr. Denis, 3" long. Parry Vieille, mark 1. $245.

Crown, 2.5" high. Eximious, mark 1. $145.

Fairy Baby on Flower, 2.75" high, $135.

Clown, 4.5" high. $110.

Seated Clown, 3.5" high. $170.

Clown Leaning Against Lamp Post, 3" high. $105.

Pierrot, 1.75" in diameter. $100.

Clown Hat, 1.75" high. $225.

Rabbit inside Clown Hat.

Owl, 2.5" high. Parry Vieille, mark 1. $100.

Bluebird, 2.25" high. Dubarry, mark 1. $135.

Goose, 2.5" high. Parry Vieille, mark 1. $125.

Christmas Robin, 1.75" high. Parry Vieille, $130.

Butterfly, 3" high. $150.

Westie, 2" high. $100.

Cat with Cup, 2.5" high. $140.

Yellow Cat, 4" high. $155.

Kittens in Sock, 2.5" high. Dubarry, mark 1. $135.

"Herrend" Style Hare, 2.75" high.
Eximious, mark 1. $165.

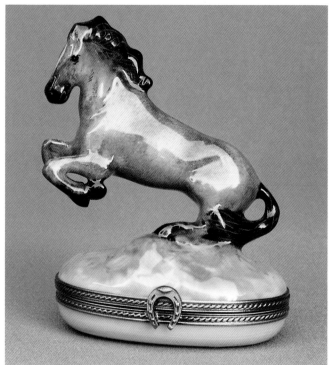

Above: Movie Rabbit, 3.25" high. $160.

Above right: Rearing Horse, 3.25" high. Parry Vieille, mark 1. $175.

Right: Asian Elephant, 2" high. Parry Vieille, mark 1. $110.

Bottom left: Friendly Frogs, 2.25" high. Dubarry, mark 1. $175.

Bottom center: Frog, 1.75" high. Parry Vieille, mark 1. $120.

Bottom right: Frogs in Love, 2.25" wide. Eximious, mark 1. $130.

White Tiger, 1.75" high. $100.

Fish, 2.5" high. Parry Vieille, mark 1. $145.

Whale, 2" high. $90.

Noah's Ark, 2.5" high. Chanille, mark 1. $190.

Blue Airplane, 3" long. $125.

Air Paradis, 4" long. $135.

London Cab, 2.75" long. Eximious, mark 1. $135.

British Phone Booth, 2.5" high. $75.

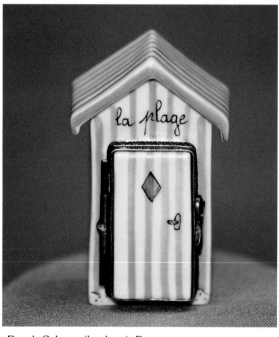

Beach Cabana (la plage). Parry Vieille, mark 1. $175.

Inside Beach Cabana.

Santa on White Sleigh, 3.5" high. $190.

Old World Snowman, 2.75" high. $90.

Rocking Horse, 3.25" long.
Parry Vieille, mark 1. $125.

Standing Santa, 4.25" high.
Limoges, mark 16. $125.

Christmas Bell, 2.75" high. $150.

Snowman, 2.75" high.
Eximious, $125.

Jack-O-Lantern, 2" in diameter. $100.

Halloween Witch, 3.75" high. $170.

Part III.

Companies and Their Marks

Over time there has been some misconception about what exactly is Limoges porcelain. While some think it refers to a specific company, it actually refers to numerous companies that produced porcelain in the Limoges region of France over the past two hundred plus years. One of the most interesting tasks for the Limoges collector is the dating and identification of porcelain makers and decorators. Marks which are under the glaze of the porcelain identify the company that manufactured the porcelain (underglaze or white ware mark). These marks are most often stamped on the porcelain, usually in green; but for older pieces especially, they may be impressed instead. Marks which are on top of the glaze identify the company that decorated, exported or imported the porcelain (overglaze mark). Without knowledge about specific companies, it is difficult to know whether a particular company was a decorator, importer or exporter or whether the company was French or American. For example, the overglaze Coronet mark indicates that the piece was imported by George Borgfeldt of New York. These items, although bearing the name of the import company, were also decorated in Limoges. On the other hand, it is somewhat easier to identify marks which name specific department stores or jewelers that imported Limoges porcelain, because the full names of the companies are stamped on the porcelain and oftentimes include the name of the city in which they are located. Also, many Americans are familiar with the names of these companies, many of which are still in business today. They include stores such as Gump's, Marshall Field & Company, Saks Fifth Avenue and Bailey, Banks and Biddle. Pieces bearing the names of the U.S. stores that imported them were also decorated in Limoges.

To date individual pieces of porcelain, the collector must know when the identifying marks were used by each particular company. This presupposes, of course, that we know the dates when each company was in business, and when each company used a particular mark. There are a number of factors that make the dating and identification of pieces difficult and why for some marks we can only approximate the dates when they were used. Factors which contribute to these difficulties are as follows:

—Many pieces of Limoges porcelain were not marked with either a manufacturing or decorating mark, especially from the time of the French Revolution at the end of 18th century to the latter half of the 19th century.

—While some pieces might have a manufacturing mark, pieces which were decorated in Limoges do not always carry a decorating mark, especially pieces decorated during the late 18th and continuing on through the 19th century. For example, to experi-

enced Limoges collectors, it is often clear that a certain piece was professionally decorated, probably in Limoges, yet there is no identifying decorating mark.

—Many Limoges manufacturers used the same underglaze mark, so it is impossible to identify the specific company which produced the porcelain, and many of these marks are very difficult to date since they cannot be associated with the history of a particular company. Dating, in these cases, is determined or approximated by the decorating mark if there is one or, if not, by the style of the decoration.

—Several companies started as just importers of Limoges porcelain, Limoges manufacturers or Limoges decorators and later expanded, but their markings do not always reflect these changes.

—There is little documentation about the histories of many of the Limoges companies, especially those that were small and those that were in existence for only a few years.

—Many of the companies merged or were taken over by other companies, and sometimes the marks of the old company were continued by the new company.

In identifying and dating the marks in this book, we have relied on numerous published sources and have used our own judgement in some cases based upon what we know of the histories of particular companies and by cross referencing underglaze and overglaze marks on the same piece of porcelain. The dating of some marks can be estimated based upon the 1891 McKinley Tariff law which required that goods imported to the U.S. list the country of origin. The Haviland companies and their corresponding marks have been well documented and are shown here as well. Dating of Le Tallec pieces is based upon a dating production chart given to us by the company. For many pieces, both old and new, the identification of the manufacturer and/or decorating company will never be known. For example, many pieces imported to the U.S. by the New York firms Lazarus Straus and Sons (LS&S) and George Borgfeldt (Coronet) include their mark and not the mark of the porcelain manufacturer or the mark of the decorating studio, if the decorating studio was another company or if the importer used more than one decorating company. We can assume that the importer used several decorating studios since many of the Limoges artists' names appear on pieces painted for several different importers. A large number of the boxes imported by Rochard bear only the *Rochard* name, with no indication of the manufacturing and decorating companies. Many of these decorating studios are, in fact, very small operations. What the *Rochard* name does tell the collector, however, is that the box was both manufactured and decorated in Limoges. Since many of the boxes on the market today are actually decorated elsewhere (e.g., Hungary, Italy and the U.S.)—

because manufacturers sell their blanks all over the world—collectors who want to be confident that they only have boxes decorated in Limoges will stick with boxes that bear the marks of well known companies or boxes that have been decorated exclusively for up-scale retail stores like Gump's in San Francisco or Lucy Zahran in Beverly Hills.

To assist the collector in following the dating of some of the marks, we have included diagrams of the histories of some of the larger and more well known Limoges companies. These diagrams indicate, for example, when certain companies were only decorating studios and later added manufacturing or vice versa and also indicate the dates when companies were bought out by other firms. Obviously, many of the marks correspond to the historical events of these companies. As stated previously, though, there are some difficulties when one firm purchases another but still continues to use the mark of the earlier firm. This is the case with the decorating mark of Charles Field Haviland, for example. The *CH FIELD HAVILAND* mark was first used by Charles Field Haviland and later by Gérard, Dufraisseix, & Morel and then finally sold to the Robert Haviland Company in 1941. Thankfully, many of these cases have been documented so that the dating of these marks are known. Finally, the dating associated with the manufacturing mark may not correspond completely with the dating of the decorating mark. This happens because the blanks were stored or sold long after the company had finished producing the blanks, sometimes up to several years later.

Limoges Manufacturers, Decorators, Exporters and Importers and Their Marks

This section on companies and their marks is organized into three sections. The first section includes primarily companies that have changed ownership, merged, spawned new companies, or otherwise have histories that help us to date their marks. The second section includes all other companies not in the first section. Finally, the third section includes marks of unidentified companies. Where possible, we have included the dates when each company was in business, and a range of dates when a given mark was used. For the dates of the companies and their marks, we have relied heavily on the published works of Jean d'Albis and Céleste Romanet, Mark Frank Gaston, Elizabeth Cameron, J. P. Cushion, and Wallace J. Tomasini and the Haviland Collectors Internationale Foundation; and we have also relied upon our own experience in cross referencing underglaze and overglaze marks and in reading other works on Limoges porcelain. Much of the information on the Limoges box companies and their marks came directly from the companies themselves. Very special thanks to Yasumasa Tanano who drew all the company marks which we were unable to photograph from actual pieces of porcelain.

Companies and Their Porcelain and Decorating Marks

AHRENFELDT

1859—C. Ahrenfeldt starts exporting firm in Limoges.

c. 1884— Ahrenfeldt starts decorating studio.

1894— Ahrenfeldt dies and his son, Charles, Junior, takes over company.

c. 1894— Company begins producing porcelain and carries on export business throughout the 1890s.

1896—M. Grob manages company.

1934—Grob dies and his wife takes over company.

1969— Company closes.

1884 to 1891

Ahrenfeldt, Mark 1, in red. Decorating mark.

c.1891 to c.1896.

Ahrenfeldt, Mark 2, in blue. Decorating mark.

Ahrenfeldt, Mark 3, in green. Decorating mark.

1894 to c.1896

Ahrenfeldt, Mark 4, in green. Porcelain mark.

c. 1896 and After

Ahrenfeldt, Mark 5, in green. Porcelain mark.

Ahrenfeldt, Mark 6, in green or gold. Decorating mark.

Ahrenfeldt, Mark 7, in green. Porcelain mark.

Ahrenfeldt, Mark 8, in green. Decorating mark.

Ahrenfeldt, Mark 9, in green. Porcelain mark.

Ahrenfeldt, Mark 10, in green. Porcelain mark.

Ahrenfeldt, Mark 11, in green. Porcelain mark.

c. 1940s and After

Ahrenfeldt, Mark 12, in blue. Decorating mark.

Ahrenfeldt, Mark 13. Decorating mark.

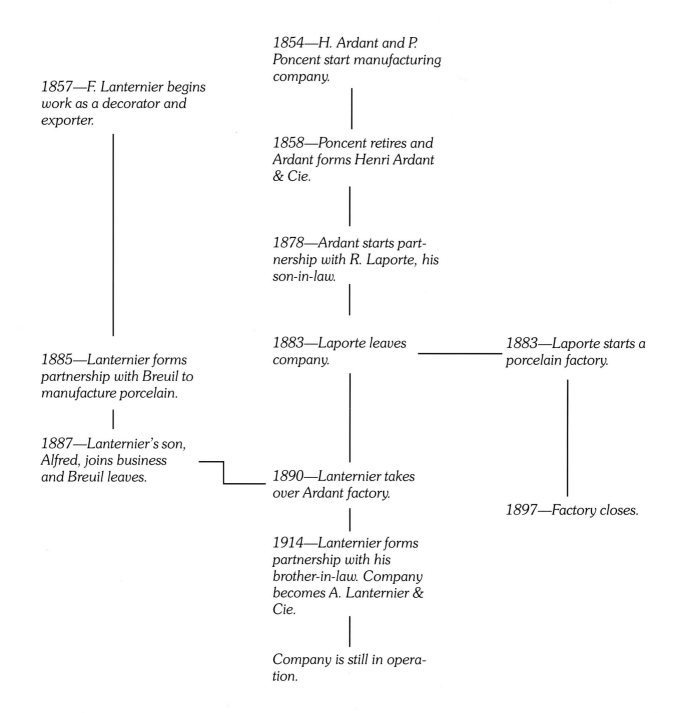

1854—H. Ardant and P. Poncent start manufacturing company.

1857—F. Lanternier begins work as a decorator and exporter.

1858—Poncent retires and Ardant forms Henri Ardant & Cie.

1878—Ardant starts partnership with R. Laporte, his son-in-law.

1883—Laporte leaves company.

1883—Laporte starts a porcelain factory.

1885—Lanternier forms partnership with Breuil to manufacture porcelain.

1887—Lanternier's son, Alfred, joins business and Breuil leaves.

1890—Lanternier takes over Ardant factory.

1897—Factory closes.

1914—Lanternier forms partnership with his brother-in-law. Company becomes A. Lanternier & Cie.

Company is still in operation.

HENRI ARDANT (1854 TO 1878)

c. 1854

Ardant, Mark 1. Porcelain mark.

1858 or After

Ardant, Mark 2. Decorating mark.

1865–

Ardant, Mark 3. Porcelain mark.

1869–

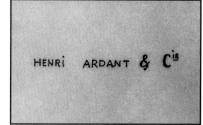

Ardant, Mark 4. Decorating mark.

RAYMOND LAPORTE (1883 TO 1897)

1883 to 1897

Laporte, Mark 1. Porcelain mark.

Laporte, Mark 2. Porcelain mark.

1891 to 1897

Laporte, Mark 3, in red. Decorating mark.

LANTERNIER (1857 TO PRESENT)

Before 1890

Lanternier, Mark 1, in blue. Decorating mark.

c. 1890

Lanternier, Mark 2, in green. Porcelain mark.

Lanternier, Mark 3, in green. Porcelain mark.

Lanternier, Mark 4, in red. Decorating mark.

1891 to 1914

Lanternier, Mark 5, in green. Porcelain mark.

Lanternier, Mark 6, in blue, red or brown. Decorating mark.

From 1914 to Present

Lanternier, Mark 7, in red and black. Decorating mark.

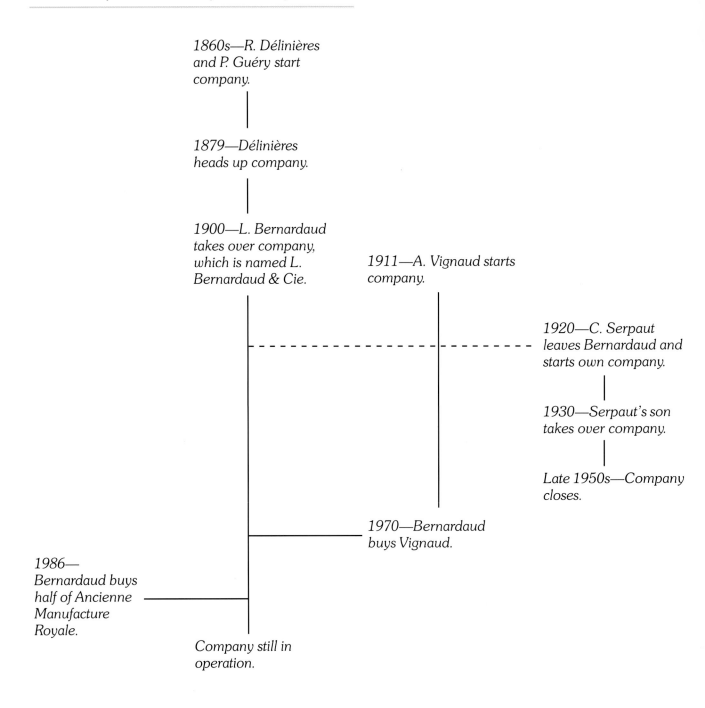

1860s—R. Délinières and P. Guéry start company.

1879—Délinières heads up company.

1900—L. Bernardaud takes over company, which is named L. Bernardaud & Cie.

1911—A. Vignaud starts company.

1920—C. Serpaut leaves Bernardaud and starts own company.

1930—Serpaut's son takes over company.

Late 1950s—Company closes.

1970—Bernardaud buys Vignaud.

1986—Bernardaud buys half of Ancienne Manufacture Royale.

Company still in operation.

R. DÉLINIÈRES & CIE (1860 TO 1900)

Before 1879

1879 to 1900

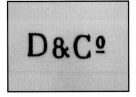

Délinières, Mark 1, in green. Porcelain mark.

Délinières, Mark 2, in green. Porcelain mark.

Délinières, Mark 3, in red. Decorating mark.

Délinières, Mark 4, in red. Decorating mark.

L. BERNARDAUD & CIE (1900 TO PRESENT)

1900–

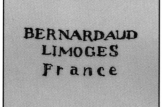

Bernardaud, Mark 1, in green. Porcelain mark.

1900 to 1929

Bernardaud, Mark 2. Decorating mark.

1900 to 1978

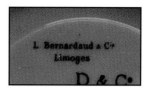

Bernardaud, Mark 3, in green. Porcelain mark.

Bernardaud, mark 4, in red. Decorating mark.

1929 to 1979+

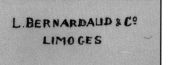

Bernardaud, Mark 5. Porcelain mark.

Used in 1969

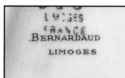

Bernardaud, Mark 6, in red. Decorating mark.

VIGNAUD (1911 TO 1970)

1911 to 1938

Vignaud, Mark 1, in green. Porcelain mark.

Vignaud, Mark 2. Decorating mark.

Vignaud, Mark 3, in green. Decorating mark.

1938 to 1970

Vignaud, Mark 4, in green. Porcelain mark.

Vignaud, Mark 5. Decorating mark.

SERPAUT (1923 TO 1950S)

1923 to 1930

Serpaut, Mark 1, in green. Porcelain mark.

After 1930

Serpaut, Mark 2. Decorating mark.

1853—P. J. Gibus with A. Margaine (formerly with Sazerat) and M. Redon start manufacturing porcelain. Business called Gibus & Cie.

1865—C. F. Haviland has rights to sell company's wares in U.S.

1872—A. Margaine leaves business, and business buys new factory. Company named Gibus & Redon.

1881/1882—Gibus retires, and Redon becomes sole owner. Company is named Martial Redon & Cie.

1894—Barny & Rigoni start manufacturing porcelain.

1896—Redon retires and brings his son, Joseph, into company.

1902—Redon joins Barny & Rigoni.

1904—Redon leaves, and Langle joins company.

1906—P. Jouhanneaud and his son join business, and company becomes La Porcelaine Limousine.

1912—G. Magnes, Jouhanneaud's nephew, becomes a partner.

1918—Magnes takes over company.

1938—Company closes.

1946—A. Chastagner reopens factory. It is named Société Chastagner.

Gibus & Cie (1853 to 1872)

1853 to 1872

Gibus, Mark 1. Porcelain mark.

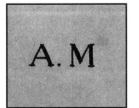

Gibus, Mark 2, A. Margaine's association with Gibus. Porcelain mark.

Gibus & Redon (1872 to 1881)

1872 to 1881

Gibus & Redon, Mark 1, impressed. Porcelain mark.

MARTIAL REDON & CIE (1882 TO 1896)

c. 1882

Redon, Mark 1, in red. Decorating mark.

1882 to 1890

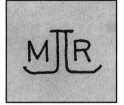

Redon, Mark 2, in green. Porcelain mark.

1882 to 1896

Redon, Mark 3, in red or blue, also used later by La Porcelaine Limousine. Decorating mark.

Redon, Mark 4, in red. Decorating mark.

1891 to 1896

Redon, Mark 5, in green. Porcelain mark.

BARNY & RIGONI (1894 TO 1906)

1849 to 1902

Barny & Rigoni, Mark 1. Porcelain mark.

1902 to 1904

Barny & Rigoni, Mark 2, also probably used later by La Porcelaine Limousine. Decorating mark.

(& Langle)
1904 to 1906

Barny & Rigoni, Mark 3, in green. Porcelain mark.

Barny & Rigoni, Mark 4. Decorating mark.

PORCELAINE LIMOUSINE (C. 1906 TO C. 1938)

(c. 1906 to c. 1938)

Porcelaine Limousine, Mark 1, in green. Porcelain mark.

Porcelaine Limousine, Mark 2, in red, also used earlier by Martial Redon & Cie. Decorating mark.

Porcelaine Limousine, Mark 3, in green. Porcelain mark.

Porcelaine Limousine, Mark 4, in green. Porcelain mark.

CHASTAGNER (1946–)

From 1950–

Chastagner, Mark 1. Porcelain mark.

Chastagner, Mark 2. Decorating mark.

GRELLET, COMTE D'ARTOIS, ANCIENNE MANUFACTURE ROYALE, ALLUAUD, C.F. HAVILAND, GDM, GDA

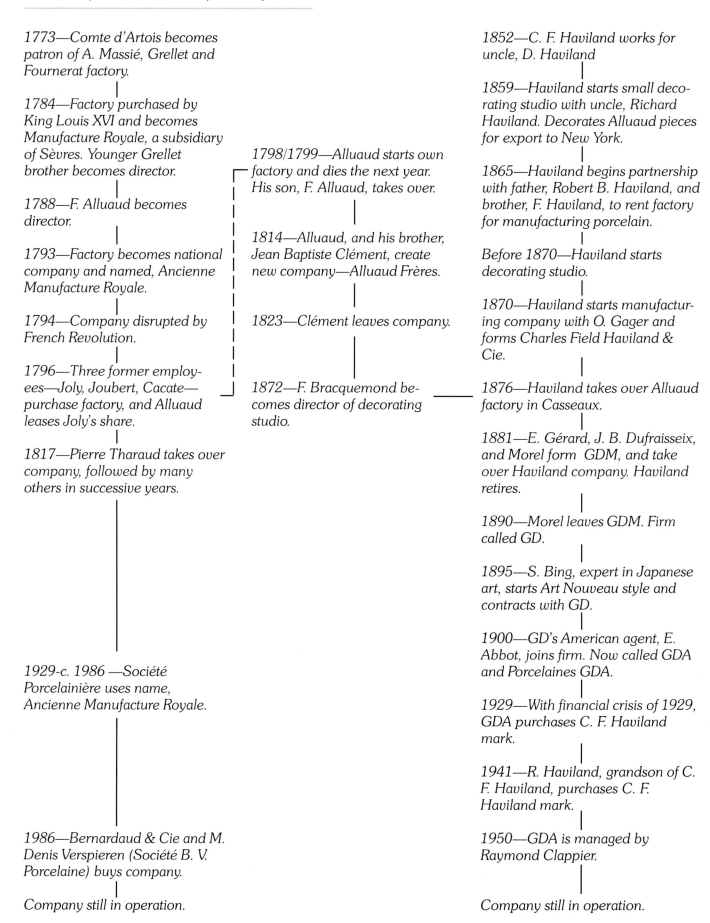

1773—Comte d'Artois becomes patron of A. Massié, Grellet and Fournerat factory.

1784—Factory purchased by King Louis XVI and becomes Manufacture Royale, a subsidiary of Sèvres. Younger Grellet brother becomes director.

1788—F. Alluaud becomes director.

1793—Factory becomes national company and named, Ancienne Manufacture Royale.

1794—Company disrupted by French Revolution.

1796—Three former employees—Joly, Joubert, Cacate—purchase factory, and Alluaud leases Joly's share.

1817—Pierre Tharaud takes over company, followed by many others in successive years.

1929-c. 1986 —Société Porcelainière uses name, Ancienne Manufacture Royale.

1986—Bernardaud & Cie and M. Denis Verspieren (Société B. V. Porcelaine) buys company.

Company still in operation.

1798/1799—Alluaud starts own factory and dies the next year. His son, F. Alluaud, takes over.

1814—Alluaud, and his brother, Jean Baptiste Clément, create new company—Alluaud Frères.

1823—Clément leaves company.

1872—F. Bracquemond becomes director of decorating studio.

1852—C. F. Haviland works for uncle, D. Haviland

1859—Haviland starts small decorating studio with uncle, Richard Haviland. Decorates Alluaud pieces for export to New York.

1865—Haviland begins partnership with father, Robert B. Haviland, and brother, F. Haviland, to rent factory for manufacturing porcelain.

Before 1870—Haviland starts decorating studio.

1870—Haviland starts manufacturing company with O. Gager and forms Charles Field Haviland & Cie.

1876—Haviland takes over Alluaud factory in Casseaux.

1881—E. Gérard, J. B. Dufraisseix, and Morel form GDM, and take over Haviland company. Haviland retires.

1890—Morel leaves GDM. Firm called GD.

1895—S. Bing, expert in Japanese art, starts Art Nouveau style and contracts with GD.

1900—GD's American agent, E. Abbot, joins firm. Now called GDA and Porcelaines GDA.

1929—With financial crisis of 1929, GDA purchases C. F. Haviland mark.

1941—R. Haviland, grandson of C. F. Haviland, purchases C. F. Haviland mark.

1950—GDA is managed by Raymond Clappier.

Company still in operation.

ANCIENNE MANUFACTURE ROYAL (1770 TO PRESENT)

Before 1774

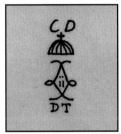

Ancienne Manufacture Royal, Mark 1. Porcelain mark.

Ancienne Manufacture Royal, Mark 2. Porcelain mark.

Beginning in 1774

Ancienne Manufacture Royal, Mark 3. Porcelain mark.

Ancienne Manufacture Royal, Mark 4. Decorating mark.

Before 1784

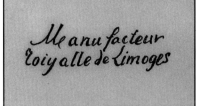

Ancienne Manufacture Royal, Mark 5.

1784 and After

Ancienne Manufacture Royal, Mark 6.

Ancienne Manufacture Royal, Mark 7.

Ancienne Manufacture Royal, Mark 8.

Ancienne Manufacture Royal, Mark 9.

(SOCIÉTÉ PORCELAINIÈRE)(1929 TO C. 1986)

Utilized in 1929

Ancienne Manufacture Royal, Mark 10. Porcelain mark.

Ancienne Manufacture Royal, Mark 11. Decorating mark.

Mark registered in 1930

Ancienne Manufacture Royal, Mark 12. Decorating mark.

Used in 1979

Ancienne Manufacture Royal, Mark 13. Porcelain mark.

Ancienne Manufacture Royal, Mark 14. Decorating mark.

Current

Ancienne Manufacture Royal, Mark 15, in gold. Decorating mark.

François Alluaud
(1798 to 1876)

Charles Field Haviland & Cie (1859 to 1881)

1881 and Before

Alluaud, Mark 1, in blue on wares dated 1867, impressed until 1881. Porcelain mark.

1881 and Before

C. F. Haviland, Mark 1, in black, brown or blue, also later used by GDM, GDA and Robert Haviland. Decorating mark.

c. 1865 to 1881

C.F. Haviland, Mark 2, impressed. Porcelain mark.

C. F. Haviland, Mark 3, in green. Porcelain mark.

C. F. Haviland, Mark 4, in black. Porcelain mark.

Gérard, Dufraisseix & Morel
(GDM)(1881 to 1890)

1881 to 1890

Gérard, Dufraisseix & Morel, Mark 1, in green. Porcelain mark.

Gérard, Dufraisseix & Morel, Mark 2, in blue, black, gray, red or brown. Decorating mark.

Gérard, Dufraisseix & Cie
(1890 to 1900)

1890 to 1900

Gérard, Dufraisseix, Mark 1, in green. Porcelain mark.

Gérard, Dufraisseix, Mark 2, in blue, black, gray, red or brown. Decorating mark.

Gérard, Dufraisseix, Abbot (GDA)(1900 to Present)

c. 1900

Gérard, Dufraisseix, Abbot, Mark 1, in green. Porcelain mark.

(Creation by Feure for Bing) c. 1900

Gérard, Dufraisseix, Abbot, Mark 2. Porcelain mark.

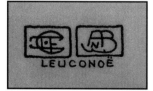

Gérard, Dufraisseix, Abbot, Mark 3. Decorating mark.

(Creation by Colonna for Bing)
c. 1900

Gérard, Dufraisseix, Abbot, Mark 4. Decorating mark.

1900 to 1941

Gérard, Dufraisseix, Abbot, Mark 5, in red, mark purchased in 1941 by Robert Haviland. Decorating mark.

1900 to 1953

Gérard, Dufraisseix, Abbot, Mark 6, in green. Porcelain mark.

1941 to 1976

Gérard, Dufraisseix, Abbot, Mark 7, in red or green. Decorating mark.

From 1970

Gérard, Dufraisseix, Abbot, Mark 8. Decorating mark.

From 1977

Gérard, Dufraisseix, Abbot, Mark 9. Decorating mark.

GUÉRIN, POUYAT, BAWO & DOTTER (ELITE)

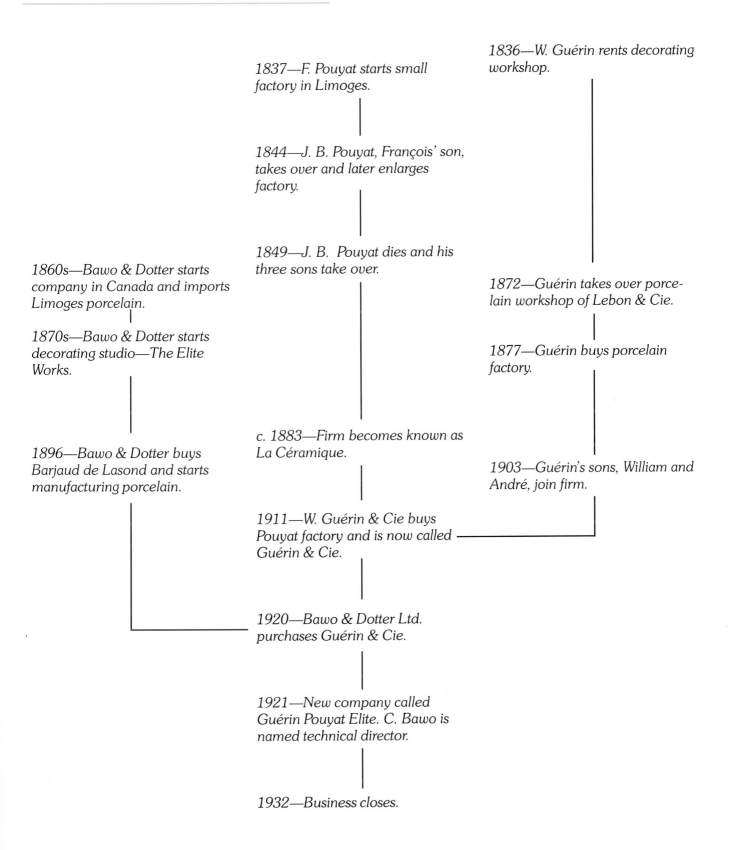

1836—W. Guérin rents decorating workshop.

1837—F. Pouyat starts small factory in Limoges.

1844—J. B. Pouyat, François' son, takes over and later enlarges factory.

1849—J. B. Pouyat dies and his three sons take over.

1860s—Bawo & Dotter starts company in Canada and imports Limoges porcelain.

1870s—Bawo & Dotter starts decorating studio—The Elite Works.

1872—Guérin takes over porcelain workshop of Lebon & Cie.

1877—Guérin buys porcelain factory.

1896—Bawo & Dotter buys Barjaud de Lasond and starts manufacturing porcelain.

c. 1883—Firm becomes known as La Céramique.

1903—Guérin's sons, William and André, join firm.

1911—W. Guérin & Cie buys Pouyat factory and is now called Guérin & Cie.

1920—Bawo & Dotter Ltd. purchases Guérin & Cie.

1921—New company called Guérin Pouyat Elite. C. Bawo is named technical director.

1932—Business closes.

WILLIAM GUÉRIN(1836 TO 1932)

From c. Late 1870s   **Before 1891**

Guérin, Mark 1, in green. Porcelain mark.

Guérin, Mark 2, in green. Porcelain mark.

Guérin, Mark 3, in red, very rare. Decorating mark.

1891 to 1932

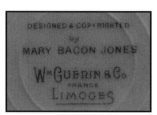

Guérin, Mark 4, in green. Porcelain mark.

Guérin, Mark 5, in blue, gold, red, green or brown. Decorating mark.

Guérin, Mark 6, in blue. Decorating mark.

Guérin, Mark 7, in blue. Decorating mark.

POUYAT (1832 TO 1932)

From 1851 to c. 1876   **c. 1876 to 1890**

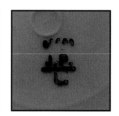

Pouyat, Mark 1, in green. Porcelain mark.

Pouyat, Mark 2, in red. Decorating mark.

Pouyat, Mark 3, in green. Porcelain mark.

Pouyat, Mark 4, in red. Decorating mark.

c. 1880s to c.1890s   **c. 1890s**   **1891 to 1932**

Pouyat, Mark 5, in red. Decorating mark.

Pouyat, Mark 6, in red. Decorating mark.

Pouyat, Mark 7, in green. Porcelain mark.

Pouyat, Mark 8, in green or in green and pink. Decorating mark.

Bawo & Dotter/The Elite Works (1860s to 1932)

c. 1870 to c. 1880s

Bawo & Dotter, Mark 1, in green or red. Decorating mark.

Bawo & Dotter, Mark 2, in red. Decorating mark.

Bawo & Dotter, Mark 3, in red. Decorating mark.

c. 1891 to 1896

Bawo & Dotter, Mark 4, in red. Decorating mark.

Bawo & Dotter, Mark 5, in red, w/ N.D.&C in shield. Decorating mark.

1896 to 1920

Bawo & Dotter, Mark 6, in green. Porcelain mark.

Bawo & Dotter, Mark 7, in red. Decorating mark.

Bawo & Dotter, Mark 8, in red. Decorating mark.

Bawo & Dotter, Mark 9, in green. Porcelain mark.

Bawo & Dotter, Mark 10, in red. Decorating mark.

Bawo & Dotter, Mark 11, in green. Porcelain mark.

Bawo & Dotter, Mark 12, in red. Decorating mark.

1920 to 1932

Bawo & Dotter, Mark 13, in red. Decorating mark.

Bawo & Dotter, Mark 14, with Guérin, Pouyat, Elite Ltd. printed inside emblem, in black and brown. Decorating mark.

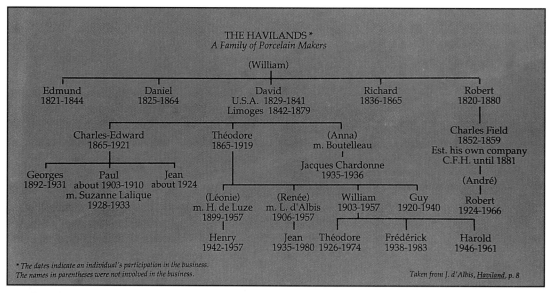

Haviland family tree. *Courtesy of Jean d'Albis.*

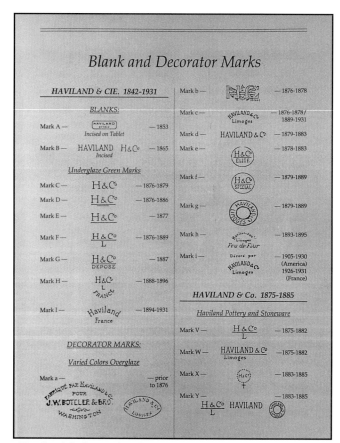

Haviland & Cie marks. *Courtesy of Haviland Collectors Internationale Foundation and Wallace J. Tomasini, Ph.D.*

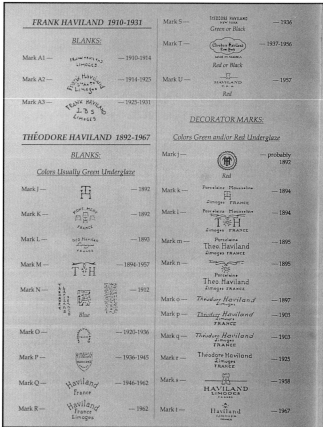

Frank and Théodore Haviland Marks and Dates. *Courtesy of Haviland Collectors Internationale Foundation and Wallace J. Tomasini, Ph.D.*

R. Haviland & C. Parlon

1924—R. Haviland starts his own porcelain company, called Robert Haviland & Cie.

1926—P. Le Tanneur joins company, which is now called Robert Haviland & Le Tanneur.

1941—R. Haviland purchases his grandfather's, C. F. Haviland, decorating mark from GDA.

1949—Le Tanneur retires from firm, and C. Parlon joins firm, which is now called Robert Haviland & C. Parlon.

Company is still in operation.

ROBERT HAVILAND (1924 TO PRESENT)

From 1924–

R. Haviland, Mark 1, in green. Porcelain mark.

R. Haviland, Mark 2. Decorating mark.

1924 to c. 1929

R. Haviland, Mark 3. Decorating mark.

(& Le Tanneur)
1929 to 1949

R. Haviland, Mark 4, in brown. Decorating mark.

From 1941–

R. Haviland, Mark 5, in red. Decorating mark.

(& C. Parlon)
From 1949–

R. Haviland, Mark 6. Decorating mark.

KLINGENBERG

1880s—A. Klingenberg operates porcelain factory and decorating studio.

Early 1900s—Klingenberg and Dwenger merge companies.

Early 1900s—C. Dwenger operates decorating studio.

1910—Company closes.

KLINGENBERG (1880S TO 1910)

1880s

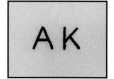

Klingenberg, Mark 1, in green. Porcelain mark.

Klingenberg, Mark 2, in red. Decorating mark.

1891 to Early 1900s

Klingenberg, Mark 3, in green. Porcelain mark.

Klingenberg, Mark 4, in red. Decorating mark.

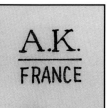

Klingenberg, Mark 5, in green. Porcelain mark.

Early 1900s to 1910

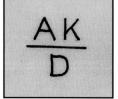

Klingenberg, Mark 6, in green. Porcelain mark.

Klingenberg, Mark 7, in red. Decorating mark.

Klingenberg, Mark 8, in green. Porcelain mark.

Klingenberg, Mark 9, in green. Porcelain mark.

Latrille, Mavaleix & Granger, Balleroy

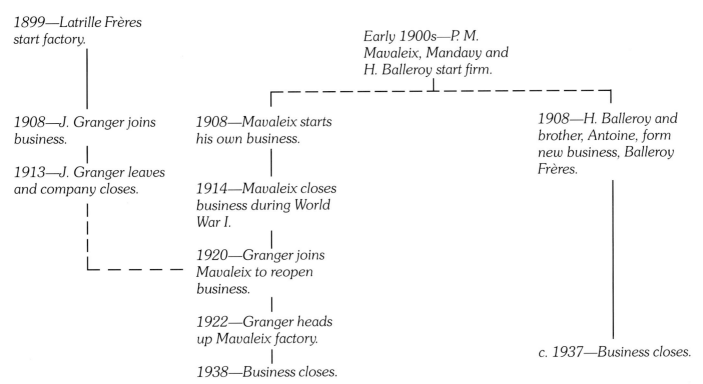

1899—Latrille Frères start factory.

Early 1900s—P. M. Mavaleix, Mandavy and H. Balleroy start firm.

1908—J. Granger joins business.

1908—Mavaleix starts his own business.

1908—H. Balleroy and brother, Antoine, form new business, Balleroy Frères.

1913—J. Granger leaves and company closes.

1914—Mavaleix closes business during World War I.

1920—Granger joins Mavaleix to reopen business.

1922—Granger heads up Mavaleix factory.

1938—Business closes.

c. 1937—Business closes.

Latrille Frères (1899 to 1913)

1899 to 1913

Latrille, Mark 1, in green. Porcelain mark.

Latrille, Mark 2, in red. Decorating mark.

1908 to 1913

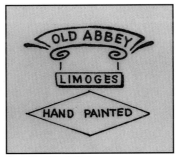

Latrille, Mark 3, in green. Decorating mark.

Latrille, Mark 4, in black and red; may instead be H. Créange mark. Decorating mark.

P. M. de Mavaleix (1908 to 1914)

P. M. de Mavaleix & Granger (1920 to 1938)

Balleroy Frères (1908 to c. 1937)

1908 to 1914

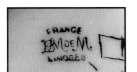

Mavaleix, Mark 1, in green. Porcelain mark.

1920 to 1938

Mavaleix & Granger, Mark 1, in green. Porcelain mark.

Mavaleix & Granger, Mark 2, in green. Porcelain mark.

Starting in 1908 or 1912 to c. 1937

Balleroy, Mark 1, in green. Porcelain mark.

Balleroy, Mark 2. Decorating mark.

1895—Mme Vue Paroutaud and her two sons, Pierre and Paul, start manufacturing company.

1902—Paroutaud Frères take over company.

1916—Paroutaud Frères leave and company becomes Maigner & Cie and is managed by A. François.

1928—Company becomes Union Porcelainière with Demarty & H. Lafarge as principals.

1941—Lafarge and N. Nardon create Limoges Porcelaine.

1963—Company becomes Porcelaine Lafarge.

Paroutaud Frères (1902 to 1916)

1903 to 1919

Paroutaud, Mark 1, in green. Porcelain mark.

Paroutaud, Mark 2. Decorating mark.

Paroutaud, Mark 3, in green. Porcelain mark.

Union Porcelainière (1928 to 1963)

1928 to 1940   **1928 to 1963**

Union Porcelainière, Mark 1. Porcelain mark.

Union Porcelainière, Mark 2. Decorating mark.

Nardon & Lafarge (1941 to 1963)

1941 to 1963

Nardon & Lafarge, Mark 2. Decorating mark.

Nardon & Lafarge, Mark 1. Decorating mark.

Lafarge (1963 to Present)

From 1963   **From 1976**

Lafarge, Mark 1. Porcelain mark.

Lafarge, Mark 2. Decorating mark.

Lafarge, Mark 3. Decorating mark.

1852—L. Sazerat starts manufacturing company with A. Margaine. —— *1853—A. Margaine leaves and joins P. J. Gibus.* —— *1881—Sazerat starts partnership with P. Blondeau.* —— *1891—Sazerat dies. Pichonnier and Duboucheron join Blondeau.* —— *1906—T. Haviland buys company and turns it into a decorating studio.*

L. SAZERAT (1852 TO 1891)

Before 1891

Sazerat, Mark 1, incised and in green. Porcelain mark.

Sazerat, Mark 2, in red. Decorating mark.

BLONDEAU, PICHONNIER AND DUBOUCHERON (1891 TO 1906)

1891 and After

Blondeau et al., Mark 1, in green. Porcelain mark.

Blondeau et al., Mark 2, in red. Decorating mark.

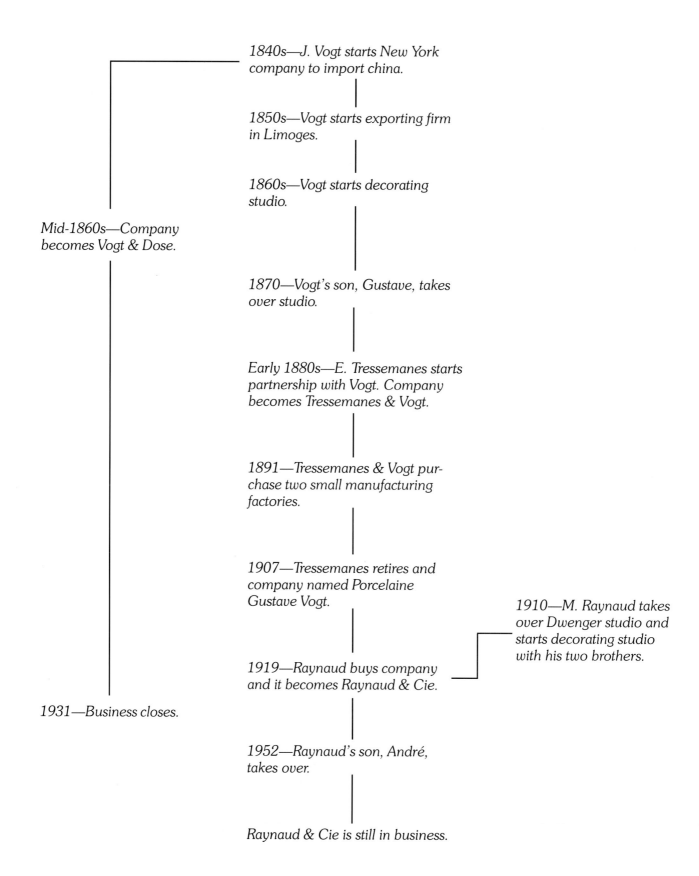

1840s—J. Vogt starts New York company to import china.

1850s—Vogt starts exporting firm in Limoges.

1860s—Vogt starts decorating studio.

Mid-1860s—Company becomes Vogt & Dose.

1870—Vogt's son, Gustave, takes over studio.

Early 1880s—E. Tressemanes starts partnership with Vogt. Company becomes Tressemanes & Vogt.

1891—Tressemanes & Vogt purchase two small manufacturing factories.

1907—Tressemanes retires and company named Porcelaine Gustave Vogt.

1910—M. Raynaud takes over Dwenger studio and starts decorating studio with his two brothers.

1919—Raynaud buys company and it becomes Raynaud & Cie.

1931—Business closes.

1952—Raynaud's son, André, takes over.

Raynaud & Cie is still in business.

Tressemanes & Vogt (Early 1880s to 1907)

Early 1880s to 1891

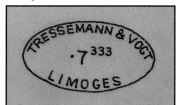

Tressemanes & Vogt, Mark 1, in blue. Decorating mark.

Tressemanes & Vogt, Mark 1.1, in purple. Decorating mark.

Tressemanes & Vogt, Mark 2, in red, purple or gold. Decorating mark.

c. 1891

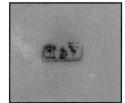

Tressemanes & Vogt, Mark 3, in green

1892 to 1907

Tressemanes & Vogt, Mark 4, in green. Porcelain mark.

Tressemanes & Vogt, Mark 5, in red or gold. Decorating mark.

Tressemanes & Vogt, Mark 6, in green. Porcelain mark.

Tressemanes & Vogt, Mark 7, in red, purple, gold or brown. Decorating mark.

Tressemanes & Vogt, Mark 8, in green. Porcelain mark.

Tressemanes & Vogt, mark 8.1, in green. Porcelain mark.

Tressemanes & Vogt, Mark 9, in green. Porcelain mark.

Tressemanes & Vogt, Mark 10, in green. Porcelain mark.

Gustave Vogt (1907 to 1919)

1907 to 1919

Tressemanes & Vogt, Mark 11, in green. Porcelain mark.

Tressemanes & Vogt, Mark 12, in purple or red. Decorating mark.

Tressemanes & Vogt, Mark 13, in purple. Decorating mark.

Tressemanes & Vogt, Mark 14. Decorating mark.

GUSTAVE VOGT (1907 TO 1919) CONTINUED

1907 to 1919 (continued)

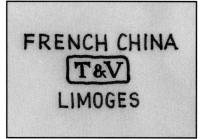

Tressemanes & Vogt, Mark 15, in red. Decorating mark.

Tressemanes & Vogt, Mark 16, in purple. Decorating mark.

Tressemanes & Vogt, Mark 17, in purple. Decorating mark.

MARTIAL RAYNAUD & CIE (1910 TO 1952)

1910 to 1919

1920s to 1930s

Raynaud, Mark 1. Decorating mark.

Raynaud, Mark 2, in green. Porcelain mark.

Raynaud, Mark 3, in purple. Decorating mark.

ANDRÉ RAYNAUD (1952 TO PRESENT)

1952 to 1960

From 1952 (used in 1979)

Raynaud, Mark 4. Porcelain mark.

Raynaud, Mark 5. Decorating mark.

Raynaud, Mark 6. Porcelain mark.

Raynaud, Mark 7, in blue. Decorating mark.

From 1960 (Also used in 1979)

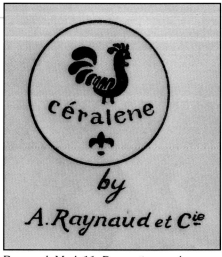

Raynaud, Mark 8. Porcelain mark.

Raynaud, Mark 9. Decorating mark.

Raynaud, Mark 10. Porcelain mark.

Raynaud, Mark 11. Decorating mark.

Aluminite René Frugier (1899 to 1964)

c. 1920s

Frugier, Mark 1.
Porcelain mark.

1936+

Frugier, Mark 2.
Porcelain mark.

c. 1950s

Frugier, Mark 3.
Porcelain mark.

From 1964 (company now part of Haviland)

Frugier/Haviland, Mark 4.
Porcelain mark.

Artoria

From 1982

Artoria, Mark 1, in green, used only on boxes decorated with transfers and boxes sold to other companies for decoration. Porcelain mark.

Artoria, Mark 2, in black.
Decorating mark.

Artoria, Mark 3, in black.
Decorating mark.

Current

Artoria, Mark 4, in gold.
Decorating mark.

Julien Balleroy & Cie

1914+

Balleroy, Mark 1.
Porcelain mark.

Bassett (U.S. Importer)

Late 1800s to WW I

Bassett, Mark 1, in red or green. Decorating mark.

Beulé, Reboisson & Parot

Beulé, Mark 1.
Porcelain mark.

BLAKEMAN & HENDERSON

BLANCHARD FRÈRES

BOISBERTRAND & THEILLOUD (1882 TO 1902)
BOISBERTRAND & DORAT (1902 TO LATE 1930S)

c. 1890s

Blakeman & Henderson, Mark 1, in green. Decorating mark.

Blakeman & Henderson, Mark 2, in red, green or gray. Decorating mark.

1890 to 1908

Blanchard, Mark 1. Decorating mark.

c. 1929

Boisbertrand, Mark 1, in green. Porcelain mark.

GEORGE BORGFELDT
(1881 TO C. 1976, U. S. IMPORTER)

1900s to c. 1920

After 1920

Borgfeldt, Mark 1, in green or blue. Decorating mark.

Borgfeldt, Mark 2, in green. Decorating mark.

JEAN BOYER (C. 1919 TO 1934)

1919–

1919 to 1934

1920 to 1934

J. Boyer, Mark 1, in blue. Decorating mark.

J. Boyer, Mark 2, in green. Porcelain mark.

J. Boyer, Mark 3, in blue. Decorating mark.

GEORGES BOYER (1934 TO PRESENT)

1934 to 1953

1939-1962

From 1953

Used in 1979

G. Boyer, Mark 1. Decorating mark.

G. Boyer, Mark 2. Decorating mark.

G. Boyer, Mark 3, in black. Decorating mark.

G. Boyer, Mark 4. Porcelain mark.

BROUSSAUD

Used in 1979

Broussaud, Mark 1.
Decorating mark.

CHABROL FRÈRES & POIRIER (1917 TO 1930s)

Used in 1929

Chabrol, Mark 1.
Porcelain mark.

CHAMART (CHARLES MARTINE) (1955 to Present)

Chamart, Mark 1, in black. Decorating mark.

CHANILLE

Late 1900s

Chanille, Mark 1.
Decorating mark.

CHAPUS & SES FILS (MANUFACTURE PORCELAINIÈRE LIMOUSINE) (1928 TO 1933)

1928 to 1933

Chapus, Mark 1.
Porcelain mark.

Chapus, Mark 2.
Decorating mark.

Chapus, Mark 3.
Decorating mark.

CHAPUS FRÈRES (1933–)

Used in 1933

Chapus, Mark 4.
Porcelain mark.

Chapus, Mark 5.
Decorating mark.

CHAPUS

Beginning in 1974 used by A. Raynaud

Chapus/Raynaud, Mark 1.
Porcelain mark.

CHAUFFRIASSE & ROUGERIE (C. 1925 TO MID-1930s)

Used in 1929

Chauffriasse, Mark 1.
Porcelain mark.

Chauffriasse, Mark 2.
Decorating mark.

L. & E. (Junior) Coiffe
(1870s to Mid-1920s)

Before 1891

Coiffe, Mark 1, in green.
Porcelain mark.

After 1891

Coiffe, Mark 2,
in green.
Porcelain mark.

Coiffe, Mark 3,
in green.
Porcelain mark.

c. 1914 to Mid-1920s

Coiffe, Mark 4,
in green.
Porcelain mark.

Coquet & Cie (1940–)

About 1964

Coquet, Mark 1.
Decorating mark.

Used in 1979

Coquet, Mark 2.
Decorating mark.

Henry Créange

c. 1907 to 1914

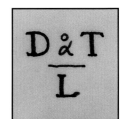

Créange, Mark 1.
Porcelain mark.

Demartial & Tallandier

1867 to 1883

Demartial, Mark 1.
Decorating mark.

Gustave Demartial

1883 to 1893

Demartial, Mark 2, in green.
Porcelain mark.

Demartial, Mark 3, in blue
green. Decorating mark.

Descottes, Reboisson & Baranger

1922 to 1927

Descottes, Mark 1.
Porcelain mark.

Dubarry

Late 1900s

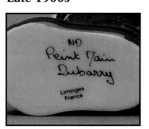

Dubarry, Mark 1, in black
or green. Decorating mark.

Eximious

From 1982

Eximious, Mark 1.
Decorating mark.

Fabergé

Late 1900s

Fabergé, Mark 1, in
gold. Decorating mark.

FLAMBEAU CHINA (L. D. B. & C.)
(C. LATE 1890s TO C. WW I)
c. Late 1890s to c. WW I

Flambeau, Mark 1, in green. Porcelain mark.

Flambeau, Mark 2, in red. Decorating mark.

Flambeau, Mark 3, in green. Decorating mark.

Flambeau, Mark 4, in green. Decorating mark.

Flambeau, Mark 5, in green, red or blue. Decorating mark.

FLORENCE

Used in 1979

Flambeau, Mark 6, in green. Decorating mark.

Flambeau, Mark 7, in green. Decorating mark.

Florence, Mark 1. Decorating mark.

FONTANILLE & MARRAUD (PORCELAINE ARTISTIQUE)
(MID-1930s TO 1980s+)
Mid-1930s and After

Used in 1979 and After

MADE IN
F LIMOGES M
FRANCE

Fontanille, Mark 1. Decorating mark.

Fontanille, Mark 2. Decorating mark.

Fontanille, Mark 3. Decorating mark.

Fontanille, Mark 4. Porcelain mark.

Fontanille, Mark 5. Decorating mark.

Fontanille, Mark 6, in brown and gold. Decorating mark.

André François (1919 to 1934)

1919 to 1934

François, Mark 1, in green. Porcelain mark.

French Accents (1983 to Present)

Current

Accents, Mark 1, in black. Decorating mark.

French & Pacific Trading Corporation (La Gloriette)

Current

Gloriette, Mark 1, in black. Decorating mark.

A. Giraud (1920s to Present)

1920s and Used in 1979

Giraud, Mark 1, in green. Porcelain mark.

Giraud, Mark 2, in green. Porcelain mark.

(with Brousseau)
1935 to 1967

Giraud, Mark 3, in blue. Decorating mark.

Used in 1979

Giraud, Mark 4. Decorating mark.

After 1979

Giraud, Mark 5. Decorating mark.

Goumot-Labesse (1954 to 1979+)

1955 to 1977

Goumot, Mark 1. Decorating mark.

(Tharaud) **From 1977**

Goumot/Tharaud, Mark 1. Decorating mark.

Oscar Gutherz (Late 1800s)

Late 1800s

Gutherz, Mark 1, in red. Decorating mark.

Gutherz, Mark 2, in red. Decorating mark.

Frank Haviland (1910 to 1924)

1910 to 1924

F. Haviland, Mark 1, in red. Decorating mark.

F. Haviland, Mark 2, in red. Decorating mark.

F. Haviland, Mark 3. Decorating mark.

JAMMET & SEIGNOLLES (1950–)

Used in 1979

Jammet, Mark 1.
Decorating mark.

LA SEYNIE-ST. YRIEIX

1775 to 1789

La Seynie, Mark 1.
Decorating mark.

La Seynie, Mark 2.
Decorating mark.

1789 to 1797

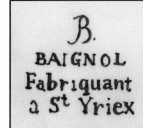

La Seynie, Mark 3.
Decorating mark.

LAVIOLETTE (1896 TO 1905)

1896 to 1905

Laviolette, Mark 1.
Porcelain mark.

LAZEYRAS, ROSENFELD & LEHMAN (1920s–)

1920s

Lazeyras, Rosenfeld & Lehman, Mark 1, in blue or red. Decorating mark.

Lazeyras, Rosenfeld & Lehman, Mark 2, in red. Decorating mark.

Lazeyras, Rosenfeld & Lehman, Mark 3, in green or gray. Decorating mark.

LE TALLEC (1930 TO PRESENT)

1930–

Le Tallec, Mark 1, used to cover name of porcelain manufacture. Decorating mark.

Before 1941

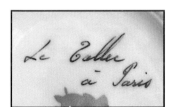

Le Tallec, Mark 2. Decorating mark.

1941 to Present

Le Tallec, Mark 3. Decorating mark.

Le Tallec Marks and Production Dates, 1941 to Present. Part of decorating marks.

DATE PRODUCTION CHART

A	B	C	D	E	F	G	H	I	J	K	L	M	
1941	1941	1942	1942	1943	1943	1944	1944	1945	1945	1946	1946	1947	13 VILLA FAUCHEUR

N	O	P	Q	R	S	T	U	V	W	X	Y	Z
1947	1948	1948	1949	1949	1950	1950	1951	1951	1952	1952	1953	1953

AA	BB	CC	DD	EE	FF	GG	HH	II	JJ	KK	LL	MM
1954	1954	1955	1955	1956	1956	1957	1957	1958	1958	1959	1959	1960

NN	OO	PP	QQ	RR	SS	TT	UU	VV	WW	XX	YY	ZZ
1960	1961	1961	1962	1962	1963	1963	1964	1964	1965	1965	1966	1966

α	β	γ	δ	ε	ζ	η	θ	ι	κ	λ	μ	ν
1967	1967	1968	1968	1969	1969	1970	1970	1971	1971	1972	1972	1973

ς	π	ρ	σ6	τ	υ	φ	χ	ψ	ω	RA	RB	RC	
1973	1974	1974	1975	1975	1976	1976	1977	1977	1978	1978	1979	1979	67 RUE DE REUILLY

RD	RE	RF	RG	RH	RI	RJ	RK	RL	RM	RN	RO	RP
1980	1980	1981	1981	1982	1982	1983	1983	1984	1984	1985	1985	1986

RQ	RR	RS	RT	RU	RV	RW	RX	RY	RZ	RRA	RRB	RRC
1986	1987	1987	1988	1988	1989	1989	1990	1990	1991	1991	1992	1993

RRD	RRE	DA	DB	DC	DD	DE	DF	DG	DH	DI	DJ	DK	
1994	1995	1995	1996	1997	1998	1999	2000	2001	2002	2003	2004	2005	93–95 AVENUE DAUMESNIL

DL	DM	DN	DO	DP	DQ	DR	DS	DT	DU	DV	DW	DX
2006	2007	2008	2009	2010	2011	2012	2013	2014	2015	2016	2017	2018

DY	DZ
2019	2020

LECLAIR (1945–)

Used in 1979

Leclair, Mark 1.
Porcelain mark.

F. LEGRAND & CIE (1904 TO 1962+, ASSOCIATED WITH BETOULE, C. 1910)

Used in 1919

Legrand, Mark 1, in
green. Porcelain mark.

1923 to 1944

Legrand, Mark 2.
Decorating mark.

P. H. LEONARD (1890S TO WW I, U.S. IMPORTER)

1890s to WW I

Leonard, Mark 1,
in red, blue or gray.
Decorating mark.

LESME (C. 1852 TO C. 1881)

1852 to c. 1881

Lesme, Mark 1.
Porcelain mark.

Lesme, Mark 2.
Decorating mark.

Lesme, Mark 3.
Porcelain mark.

LEVY (LATE 1800S TO EARLY 1900S)

Late 1800s to Early 1800s

Levy, Mark 1, in
red. Decorating
mark.

LIMOGES CASTEL (1944 TO 1980+)

1944 to 1973

Castel, Mark 1.
Decorating mark.

Used in 1955 to 1979+

Castel, Mark 2.
Porcelain mark.

Used in 1979

Castel,
Mark 3.
Decorating
mark.

SIGMUND MAAS (1894 TO C. 1930)

Maas, Mark 1, in
red or blue.
Decorating mark.

E. MADESCLAIREX (UNTIL 1934)

Used in 1929

Madesclaire, Mark 1.
Decorating mark.

MANUFACTURE NOUVELLE DE PORCELAINE (1960 TO 1978+)

Used in 1979

Nouvelle, Mark 1,
in green. Porcelain
mark.

Nouvelle, Mark 2.
Decorating mark.

CHARLES MARTIN & DUCHÉ (1880s TO 1935)

After 1891

Martin, Mark 1, in green. Porcelain mark.

Martin, Mark 2. Porcelain mark.

Used in 1929

Martin, Mark 3. Porcelain mark.

Martin, Mark 4, in green or blue. Decorating mark.

MERIGOUS

From 1978

Merigous, Mark 1. Porcelain mark.

Merigous, Mark 2. Decorating mark.

P. MERLIN-LEMAS

Mid-1920s+

Merlin, Mark 1. Porcelain mark.

Merlin, Mark 2. Decorating mark.

L. MICHELAUD (1908 TO 1962)

After 1918   **1920s**

Michelaud, Mark 1, in blue. Decorating mark.

Michelaud, Mark 2, in black. Decorating mark.

MIAUTRE, RAYNAUD & CIE (1929 TO 1934)

1929+

Miautre, Mark 1. Porcelain mark.

PAIRPOINT (U.S. DECORATING COMPANY)

c.1880s

Pairpoint, Mark 1. Decorating mark.

CESAR PALMA (1990s)

Palma, Mark 1, in black. Porcelain mark.

L. Parant (1863 to 1868)

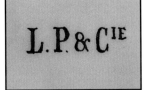

Parant, Mark 1, impressed. Porcelain mark.

P. PASTAUD (1920s TO 1950s)

Pastaud, Mark 1, in gold. Decorating mark.

Pastaud, Mark 2, in green. Porcelain mark.

A. PILLIVUYT
(1913 TO 1936)
Used in 1929

Pillivuyt, Mark 1.
Porcelain mark.

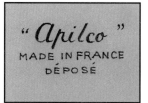

Pillivuyt, Mark 2.
Decorating mark.

PLAINE MAISON FRÈRES
(C. 1890S TO C. 1910)

Plaine Maison,
Mark 1, in green.
Porcelain mark.

PORCELAINE BLANCHE

Used in 1979

Blanche,
Mark 1.
Decorating
mark.

PORCELAINERIE DE LA HAUTE-VIENNE
(1920 TO 1959)
1920 to 1959

Haute-Vienne,
Mark 1. Porcelain
mark.

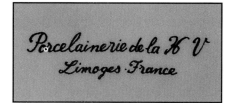

Haute-Vienne, Mark 2.
Decorating mark.

PORCELAINE INDUSTRIELLE
DU LIMOUSIN
Used in 1979 and Current

Industrielle, Mark 1, in
green. Porcelain mark.

PORCELAINE PALLAS

1926 to 1950

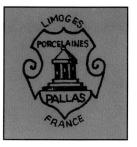

Pallas, Mark 1.
Decorating mark.

ANDRÉ PREVOT
(1952–)
Used in 1979

Prevot, Mark 1.
Decorating mark.

CHARLES REBOISSON
(1942–)

Reboisson, Mark 1.
Decorating mark.

RIFFATERRE

c. 1900

Riffaterre, Mark 1.
Decorating mark.

ROCHARD
(1972 TO PRESENT)

Rochard, Mark 1, in
black. Decorating mark.

Rochard, Mark
2, in black.
Decorating mark.

ROUSSET & GUILLEROT

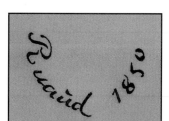

Rousset, Mark 1. Porcelain
mark./Decorating mark.

RUAUD
(1850S TO 1869)

Ruaud, Mark 1.
Porcelain mark.

SCOTLAND'S YARD STUDIO

Late 1900s

Scotland's Yard, Mark
1. Decorating mark.

Siegel & Sohm (1906 to 1923)

1920 to 1923

Siegel, Mark 1.
Porcelain mark.

Siegel, Mark 2.
Decorating mark.

Singer

1954 to 1974

Singer, Mark 1.
Decorating mark.

Lazarus Straus & Sons
(c. 1890s to c. Mid-1920s, U.S. importer)

c. 1890s to c. Mid-1920s

Lazarus Straus &
Sons, Mark 1, in blue,
red, green or gray.
Decorating mark.

Jules Teissonnière
(1908 to 1940s)

Used in 1929

Teissonnière, Mark 1.
Decorating mark.

Dates Uncertain

Teissonnière, Mark 2.
Decorating mark.

L. Téxeraud
(1923 to c. 1930)

c. 1920s

Téxeraud, Mark 1.
Decorating mark.

Téxeraud, Mark 2.
Decorating mark.

Used in 1929

Téxeraud, Mark 3.
Decorating mark.

H. Thabard
(1932 to c.1950)

1932 to c.1950

Thabard, Mark 1.
Decorating mark.

Camille Tharaud
(1920 to 1968)

1920+

Tharaud, Mark 1,
impressed. Porcelain mark.

Tharaud, Mark 2, in green,
blue, or gold. Without
Limoges France, 1920s;
with *Limoges France*, after
1920s. Decorating mark.

Tharaud, Mark 3.
Porcelain mark.

Thomas

Used in 1979

Thomas, Mark 1.
Decorating mark.

Touze, Lemaître & Blancher
(1918 to 1939)

Touze, Mark 1.
Porcelain mark.

Turgot

Current

Turgot, Mark 1.
Porcelain mark.

Union Céramique
(1909 to 1938)

1909 to 1938

Union Céramique, Mark 1, in green. Porcelain mark.

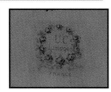

Union Céramique, Mark 2, in red. Decorating mark.

Union Limousine
(1908 to Present)

Prior to 1950

Union Limousine, Mark 1. Porcelain mark.

1950 to 1975

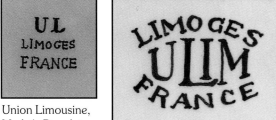

Union Limousine, Mark 2. Porcelain mark.

Union Limousine, Mark 3. Porcelain mark.

Used in 1979

Union Limousine, Mark 4. Porcelain mark.

Parry Vieille

Current

Vieille, Mark 1, in black. Decorating mark.

Villegoureix
(c. 1919 to Mid-1920s)

c. 1920s

Villegoureix, Mark 1.

Vultury Frères
(1897 to 1904)

1897 to 1904

Vultury, Mark 1, in green. Porcelain mark.

A&D

1891+

A&D, Mark 1, in green or red. Decorating mark.

AJCO

c. 1930s and After

AJCO, Mark 1, in blue. Decorating mark.

AV

1880s

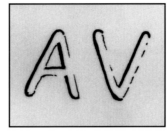

AV, Mark 1, impressed, may be Aragon and Vultury. Porcelain mark.

BEAUX-ARTS

c. 1900

Beaux-Arts, Mark 1, in green. Decorating mark.

B.H.

1920s and Earlier

B.H., Mark 1, in green, possibly Blakeman & Henderson. Porcelain mark.

B.S.

c. 1920s

B.S., Mark 1, in green. Decorating mark.

C.H.

1920s+

C.H., Mark 1, in green, probably a Bawo & Dotter mark. Porcelain mark.

C. ET J.

c. 1890s to c. 1920s

C. et J., Mark 1, in red. Decorating mark.

CMC OR GMC

After 1891

CMC, Mark 1, in green. Porcelain mark.

COMTE D'ARTOIS

Late 1900s

Artois, Mark 1, in blue. Decorating mark.

E.G.D.&CO.

c. 1890s

E.G.D.&Co., Mark 1, in green. Decorating mark.

FLORALE

c. 1920s

Florale, Mark 1, in green. Decorating mark.

GC

Late 1900s

GC, Mark 1, in black. Decorating mark.

H&C

Late 1800s

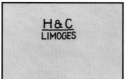

H&C, Mark 1, in green, not Haviland & Co. mark . Porcelain mark.

J.B.

Late 1900s

J.B., Mark 1, in brown. Porcelain mark.

JMcD&S
(1880s to WW I, U.S. Importer/retailer)

1880s to 1890

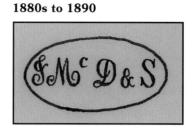

JMcD&S, Mark 1, in red. Decorating mark.

c. 1891 to WW I

JMcD&S, Mark 2, in red. Decorating mark.

L.B.H.

c. 1890s

L.B.H., Mark 1, in red. Decorating mark.

L.R.

c. 1920s

L.R., Mark 1, in red, possibly Lazeyras, Rosenfeld & Lehman. Decorating mark.

L.R.L.

c. 1920s

L.R.L., Mark 1, in blue, possibly Lazeyras, Rosenfeld & Lehman. Decorating mark.

LIMOGES, FRANCE

c. 1891 and After

Limoges, Mark 1, in green, common to many manufacturers. Porcelain mark.

Limoges, Mark 2, in red. Porcelain mark.

Limoges, Mark 3, in green. Porcelain mark.

Limoges, Mark 4, in green, also used by Artoria. Porcelain mark.

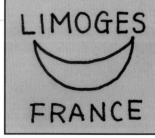

Limoges, Mark 5, in green. Porcelain mark.

Limoges, Mark 6, in green. Porcelain mark.

Limoges, Mark 7, in green. Porcelain mark.

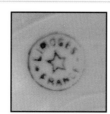

Limoges, Mark 8, in green. Porcelain mark.

Limoges, Mark 9, in green. Porcelain mark.

Limoges, Mark 10, in green. Porcelain mark.

After 1908

Adopted in 1929 by several companies

Limoges, Mark 11, in blue. Decorating mark.

Mark 12, in red. Decorating mark.

Limoges, Mark 13, in gray. Decorating mark.

Limoges, Mark 14. Porcelain mark.

LIMOGES ART PORCELAINE

Latter half of 1900s

Early 1900s

Limoges, Mark 15, in black. Decorating mark.

Limoges, Mark 16, in black. Decorating mark.

Limoges, Mark 17, in green. Porcelain mark.

Limoges Art, Mark 1, in green. Decorating mark.

ROYAL CHINA   STRAWBRIDGE & CLOTHIER   SW   VF

c. 1920s and After

After 1891

After 1891

Early 1890s

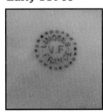

Royal China, Mark 1, in red. Decorating mark.

Strawbridge & Clothier, Mark 1, in green. Decorating mark.

VF, Mark 1, in green. Decorating mark.

SW, Mark 1, in red. Decorating mark.

OTHER   REPRODUCTIONS MADE IN TAIWAN

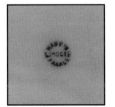

Other, Mark 1, in green, company name illegible. Porcelain mark.

Taiwan, Mark 1. Decorating mark.

Part IV.
Artists, Decorators, Retailers

French and American Artists, U.S. Decorating Studios and U.S. Retailers/Importers

We have provided the following list of French and American decorators, painters and sculptors. Those artists who are French are indicated by an asterisk (*). At times it is difficult to be certain of the spelling of an artist's name from a particular painting. In cases where we cannot be certain of the spelling of a particular name, we have included a question mark with parenthesis (?) after the name.

FRENCH AND AMERICAN DECORATORS, PAINTERS AND SCULPTORS

Ack, L.E.
Armond* (?)
Bal or Bac* (?)
Baldwin, A.F.
Baunnelly, A.
Bradford, L.B.
Broussillon, Ted Alfred (1859-1922)*
Brunner, I.L.
Buggelli, A.S.
Burcer, E.
Buzanay or Bzaranay* (?)
Carey, D.
Chambers, H.
Colean, P.
Collot, A.
Comeford, M.
Coudert, L. (decorator about 1900)*
Cummins
Curtis, Henrietta
Depitour*
Descombes, Jacob*
Descomps, Joe (sculptor for Haviland, 1869-1950)*
Dubois*
Dulac*
Duval*
Dwyer, S.F.
Farrier, M.E.
Fredy*
Fuller, E.R.
Geagren, L.
Gilbot*
Glass, E.J.
Gobse, J.
Greenaway, Kate*
Hattie
Heal, N.
Henkies* (?)
hétreau, r.*

Jean, L.*
Jones, Mark Bacon*
Jubal*
Kilbourne, Fanny H.
Lalique, Suzanne* (associated with Haviland, 1928-1933)
Lainy, E.* (?)
Larue, J.*
Leonard, L.
Levey
Luc (decorator about 1920)*
Lykes, G.
Mackenzie, M.
Marc* (?)
Marcadet
Marlin, G.S.
Martin, J.*
Mcoiscic, Y.
Meck, S.R.
Mieghorn
Miler, E.
Moch, Koch or Roch* (?)
Mongars, J.*
Morray, J.*
Morsey, J.*
Patry-Bie, S.* (associated with Haviland, 1935-1968)
Penne, E.M.
Pic, L.E.*
Price, L.P.
Prolongeau, Jean Jacques (ceramist, 1917-1994)*
Roekeloh, E.
Sandoz, Edouard*
Savine, L.* (associated with Haviland, 1907)
Shermen, Lena A.
Soustre, S.*
Stun, Cavin
Towler
Vidal, E.*
Williams, A.E.

U.S. Decorating Studios

Following are some U.S. decorating studios whose marks appear on Limoges porcelain:

The Art China Decorating Company
The Artistic Hand Painting Company
Jul. H. Brauer
Claremore Art Studio
Pairpoint, New Bedford, Massachusetts
Pickard, Chicago
Stouffer, Chicago
White's Art Company, Chicago

U.S. Retailers

There were many retailers in the U.S. which imported Limoges porcelain decorated by Limoges companies. Although the names and/or marks of these U.S. companies are often used on the porcelain instead of the mark of the Limoges decorating company, the pieces were decorated in Limoges. Following are some examples of these U.S. companies:

Abram, French & Company, Boston and Chicago
Bailey, Banks and Biddle, Philadelphia
S. & G. Gump Company (Gump's), San Francisco
H. T. Lacy & Company, Kansas City, Missouri
Marshall Field & Company, Chicago
Saks Fifth Avenue, New York
Wanamaker's, Washington, D. C.
Wright Tyndale and Van Roden, Philadelphia

Descriptions of Limoges Box Companies

We have provided a brief description of the companies involved with Limoges boxes, since there is little or no published material about them. A large proportion of Limoges boxes in the U.S. have no markings to indicate the porcelain manufacturer, the decorating studio or the distributor (exporter/importer). The reasons for this are several. Many of the distributors are very small companies and are in business for only a short period of time. There are also several companies that distribute only second- and third-rate quality boxes that are rejected by the more well know companies. Additionally, several companies distribute boxes that, in fact, are not decorated in Limoges but elsewhere and then sold in the U.S. under the pretense that they were decorated in Limoges. Many Limoges boxes do not indicate the decorating studio, primarily because most of the present day decorating studios are very small operations and are not large enough to have a company identification. Many of these small workshops decorate boxes for several of the more well known distributors, who help decide which kind of porcelain molds to produce and how they should be decorated to appeal to the U.S. market.

Listed below are the names and brief descriptions of the more well known companies:

ANCIENNE MANUFACTURE ROYALE. Ancienne Manufacture Royale began in 1737. It was started as a *faiencerie* by the Massié brothers; and after the discovery of kaolin in 1769, the Grellet brothers joined the company. It was the first manufacture to use a *Limoges* mark on its porcelain. In 1986, Ancienne Manufacture Royale was purchased equally by Bernardaud and M. Denis Verspieren. Today, Ancienne Manufacture Royale is a decorating studio, and its unique porcelain blanks are manufactured by Bernardaud.

ARTORIA. Artoria, a privately held company, is the largest giftware manufacturer in Limoges. They manufacturer Limoges box blanks, decorate them and export them to the U.S. They sell many of their blanks to other decorating studios in Limoges as well as to other companies throughout the world. The blanks, which are sold to other companies, are identified with an underglaze mark, with the word, *Limoges*, in a half-moon shape, over the word *France*. Likewise, Artoria decorated boxes that utilize transfers also carry this same underglaze mark. Artoria boxes which are entirely hand-painted only carry the mark *Artoria* and not the green ware mark. Many of the Artoria boxes include the name of the artist following the words *Exclusif* or *Exclusive*. In 1982, under its current president, Thierry de Merindol, Artoria expanded its operations to the U.S. and in 1995 opened a permanent showroom in New York City.

BERNARDAUD & CIE. Bernardaud began in 1863 and now produces a wide variety of porcelain pieces, including boxes.

CHAMART (CHARLES MARTINE). The founder of the company, Charles Martine, began importing Limoges porcelain into the U.S. in the early 1950s; and the company was officially incorporated in 1955. Mr. Martine was the first to begin importing Limoges boxes into the U.S., beginning in 1960. Today, Chamart is one of the major importers of quality Limoges boxes in the U.S. All of their boxes are totally hand-painted, many by artists who are exclusive to the company. They use no transfers or decals. While they purchase their porcelain from other Limoges companies, about half of their blanks are unique to them. The company's president, Leny Davidson, is the niece of the late Mr. Martine who died in 1996. They display approximately 2,500 boxes in their showroom in New York City.

CHANILLE. Chanille is an exporter of Limoges boxes.

DUBARRY. Based in London, Dubarry imports boxes to England and the U.S.

EXIMIOUS OF LONDON. Eximious has been importing Limoges boxes into the U.S. since 1986. They are primarily a catalogue retailer, both in the U.S. and England, with one retail outlet off Sloane Square in London. Their boxes are sold through their catalogue, *Eximious of London*. Purchasing the company's Limoges boxes directly from Limoges, France, Josephine Lewis, president of the company, states that she is involved in the design and decoration of the boxes sold through the *Eximious* catalogue. The company's boxes are marked *Eximious* and include both boxes which are all hand-painted as well as boxes that are mixed—a combination of transfers and hand-painting.

FARLIN'S. A U.S. importer of Limoges boxes.

FONTANILLE & MARRAUD. Fontanille and Marraud is a decorator that utilizes transfers with hand-painted accents. The authors have not seen any boxes that are completely hand-painted.

FRENCH ACCENTS. French Accents, located in Torrance, California, manufactures, decorates and distributes Limoges boxes. The company started in 1983; and although for a short time several years ago they used some transfers, currently all of their boxes are hand-painted.

FRENCH & PACIFIC TRADING CORPORATION. A distributor of Limoges boxes based in Chino, California. They sell boxes which are marked *La Gloriette*.

LE TALLEC. Le Tallec is a decorating studio in Paris, started in 1930 by the artist, Camille Le Tallec, who died in 1992. The company was subsequently purchased by Tiffany & Company in 1993. Using Limoges porcelain blanks, the company produces boxes, dinnerware and decorative pieces, and owns 250 patterns, which are mostly interpretations of museum pieces from the 18th and 19th centuries. Tiffany & Company owns 42 patterns that are made exclusively for them. Production dates, beginning with 1941, are marked on the bottom of each piece, as noted in the accompanying chart. Le Tallec is widely considered to be the most prestigious porcelain decorating company in France.

LIMOGES CASTEL. Limoges Castel both produced and decorated Limoges boxes. Most of their boxes are decorated with transfers, and many are deep blue with gold accents. The company is no longer in business.

PORCELAINE INDUSTRIELLE DU LIMOUSIN. This company is one of the oldest and largest Limoges porcelain manufacturers, and it is located south of Limoges in St. Yrieix.

PUY DE DOME. This company is a Limoges box distributor.

ROCHARD. Rochard is one of the largest importers of Limoges boxes to the U.S. Based in New York City, Rochard was incorporated in the fall of 1972 and initially imported traditional dinnerware and giftware from Limoges. In 1974 Rochard began importing Limoges boxes; and along with Charles Martine, introduced these boxes to the U.S. Rochard distributes many exquisitely decorated boxes.

S&D LIMOGES. Founded in 1981 by Shirley Dickerson, S&D Limoges, an importer, focuses on Limoges boxes that have a classical design or which represent themes of well known fables, fairy tales and historical objects. Although their boxes are not company marked, S&D Limoges imports some of the finest decorated Limoges boxes available in the U.S. Based in Texas, they distribute their boxes to only high end retailers.

SCOTLAND'S YARD STUDIO. Mary Scotland is a U.S. decorator of Limoges boxes.

PARRY VIEILLE. Parry Vieille, located in Limoges, is a manufacturer and decorator of boxes. They produce many well decorated boxes, which are distributed by Rochard and other companies. Although most of their boxes are entirely hand-painted, they also produce boxes that are a combination of transfers and hand-painting.

CESAR PALMA FOR HSN *(Home Shopping Network)*. We have no information on this company.

Historical Photographs

Included in this chapter are a few representative advertisements for Limoges porcelain in the U.S. and historical pictures of Limoges, France, and the making of Limoges porcelain.

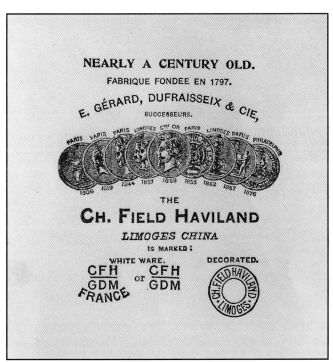

Cover of a promotional booklet published by E. Gérard, Dufraisseix & Cie (1890-1900), promoting the Brittany blank.

Advertisement for the Brittany blank.

CH. FIELD HAVILAND

LIMOGES CHINA.

18

TEA NORMANDY.
Decor. "144 Bis."

CREAM "BRITTANY."
Decor. "450 Bis."

TEAPOT BRITTANY
Decor "339 Bis."

Right: Advertisement for the Brittany blank.

Below left: Brittany game set, which includes one platter, twelve plates and two small relish dishes.

Below right: Advertisement for the Brittany blank.

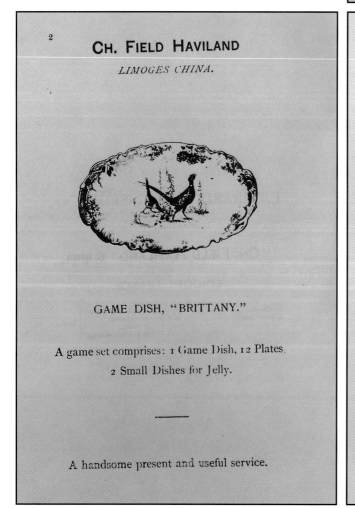

CH. FIELD HAVILAND

LIMOGES CHINA.

2

GAME DISH, "BRITTANY."

A game set comprises: 1 Game Dish, 12 Plates,
2 Small Dishes for Jelly.

———

A handsome present and useful service.

CH. FIELD HAVILAND

LIMOGES CHINA.

6

SOUP TUREEN, "BRITTANY."

Handsome Shapes and Artistic Decorations
in Dinner Services.

FISH SET, LOUIS XV.

Fish and water in natural colors. Marine
plants in gold and bronze.

Advertisement for
Pouyat China in the
March 1906 *Century*
magazine.

Applying gold decora-
tion at the Haviland
factory, from *Harper's*,
October 1888.

Filter presses for porcelain clay,
from *Harper's*, October 1888.

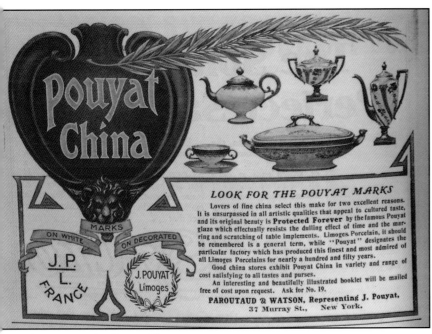

Advertisement for Pouyat China in
the May 1906 *Century* magazine.

Rue des Petits Carmes, Limoges,
from *Harper's*, October 1888.

Decorating porcelain at the P. Pastaud factory,
from a promotional flyer, early mid-1900s.

Handpainting of porcelain at the P. Pastaud factory.

The kilns for firing the decorations at the P. Pastaud factory.

Further Information

Collectors who are looking for high quality Limoges boxes may want to contact the following retailers. These stores carry some of the finest examples of decorated Limoges boxes that include truly limited editions and boxes designed exclusively for their stores:

GUMP'S. Gump's in San Francisco carries a large number of Limoges boxes, especially through their catalogue division but also in their flagship store in San Francisco. Examples of some of their exclusive pieces include an Asian foo dog, a golden buddha on a blue base and a San Francisco cable car. These pieces are all exquisitely hand-painted. Readers can contact Gump's at 135 Post Street, San Francisco, CA 941098. (Telephone: 415-982-1616).

LUCY ZAHRAN. Lucy Zahran is in Beverly Hills and Costa Mesa, California, and has a large selection of Limoges boxes and Le Tallec porcelain pieces. Lucy Zahran is one of the few stores nationwide, other than Tiffany's, that carries Le Tallec decorated porcelain. There are many Limoges boxes and Le Tallec pieces that are limited editions and exclusive to the store. The address for Lucy Zahran is 328 N. Rodeo Drive, Beverly Hills, CA 90210. (Telephone: 310-273-1338).

SCULLY & SCULLY. Scully & Scully carries Limoges boxes and a large selection of Le Tallec pieces. Scully & Scully is located at 504 Park Avenue, New York, NY 10022. (Telephone: 212-755-2590).

Readers who may wish to contact BRUCE GUILMETTE about his extensive Limoges porcelain collection can reach him at P.O. Box 822, Atkinson, NH 03811-0822.

Establishing Values for Limoges Porcelain, Including Boxes

The values we have established in this book are based on our personal observations of selling prices for like or similar pieces. Values, as we have discussed earlier, are dependent upon a number of factors, and prices vary by region of the country. One of the best sources for determining values are auctions on the world wide web because they are ongoing daily throughout the year, and bidders represent all regions of the country. However, many of the auction prices are, in a sense, wholesale prices, since many of the bidders are antique dealers who resell items at higher prices in antique malls and other outlets. As a result, we have tried to arrive at "blended" values—prices on the web, prices at swap meets and antique malls, prices at web site retail outlets, prices at antique shows and discussions with other collectors. For contemporary Limoges boxes, there is a wide variety of pricing, both within the same quality categories and between upper end and lower end boxes. For upper end boxes, some retail stores and catalogues routinely discount boxes by 20 percent, and full retail prices can vary by 10 percent or more from one high end store or catalogue to the other. Many boxes of less quality can be found on the web and are available at some discount warehouses and other retail stores, and they are also sold on television on the Home Shopping Network and QVC.

Because prices can vary substantially over time and by region and source, the values in this book should be used only as a guide. In many cases, prices on older pieces of Limoges porcelain are substantially higher on the East Coast than elsewhere in the country. We have by no means attempted to set prices for any particular items.

Bibliography

Albis, Jean d', and Céleste Romanet. *La Porcelaine de Limoges*. Paris: Sous le Vent, 1980.

Auscher, E. S. *A History and Description of French Porcelain*. Translated and Edited by William Burton. London: Cassell and Company, Ltd., 1905.

Blonston, Gary. "A Surprise in Every Box." *Arts & Antiques* (1995): 75-77.

Cameron, Elisabeth. *Encyclopedia of Pottery and Porcelain: 1800-1960*. New York: Facts on File Publications, 1986.

Chefs-d'Oeuvre de la Porcelaine de Limoges. Paris: Réunion des Musées Nationaux, 1996.

Celebrating 150 Years of Haviland China: 1842-1992. Haviland Collectors Internationale Foundation, 1992.

Child, Theodore. "Limoges and Its Industries." *Harper's New Monthly Magazine* 72 (1888): 651-664.

Cunynghame, Henry H. *European Enamels*. New York: G. P. Putnam's Sons, 1906.

Cushion, J. P., in collaboration with W. B. Honey. *Handbook of Pottery and Porcelain Marks*. 4th Edition. London: Faber and Faber, 1983.

E. Gérard, Dufraisseix & Cie. *E. Gérard, Dufraisseix & Co., Manufacturers of the "Ch. Field Haviland" China, Limoges, France*. Reprint. N.p., n.d.

Gaston, Mark Frank. *The Collector's Encyclopedia of Limoges Porcelain*. Second Edition. Paducah, Kentucky, 1994.

Kovel, Ralph M., and Terry H. Kovel. *Dictionary of Marks: Pottery and Porcelain*. New York: Crown publishers, Inc., 1953.

Kovel, Ralph, and Terry Kovel. *Kovels' New Dictionary of Marks*. New York: Crown Publishers, Inc., 1986.

Landais, Hubert. *French Porcelain*. Translated from the French by Isabel and Florence McHugh. New York: G. P. Putnam's Sons, 1961.

Mannoni, Edith. *Porcelaine de Limoges*. Paris: Massin Editeur, n.d.

Segonds, Jean-Claude. *Les Créations en Porcelaine de Limoges: D'Édouard Marcel Sandoz*. Italy: Hermé, 1995.

Travis, Nora. *Haviland China: The Age of Elegance*. Atglen, Pennsylvania: Schiffer Publishing, Ltd., 1997.

Wynter, Harriet. *An Introduction to European Porcelain*. New York: Thomas Y. Crowell Company, 1972.

Index